PROGRESSIVE FLY FISHING
FOR SALMON

PROGRESSIVE FLY FISHING

FOR SALMON

Alexander Baird Keachie

The Crowood Press

First published in 1997 by
The Crowood Press Ltd
Ramsbury, Marlborough
Wiltshire SN8 2HR

British Library Cataloguing-in-Publication Data
A catalogue record for this book is available from the British Library.

ISBN 1 86126 048 2

Photographs by the author and Mary Keachie.

Typeface used: Times.

Typeset and designed by
D & N Publishing
Membury Business Park, Lambourn Woodlands
Hungerford, Berkshire.

Printed and bound by Redwood Books.

Contents

ACKNOWLEDGEMENTS

I would like to thank the following for granting me permission to use text from their books: Hugh Falkus, author of *Salmon Fishing – A Practical Guide* (Witherby); Francis Grant, author of *Salmon Fly Fishing – The Dynamics Approach* (Swanhill Press); William B. Currie, author of *The River Within* (Merlin Unwin Books); and Derek Knowles, author of *Salmon on a Dry Fly* (Witherby, Victor Gollancz). Thanks also to Crawford Little, Arthur Oglesby and Michael Evans who allowed me to use text from articles they had published.

My appreciation to Mr Bannarjee of Veniards who supplied me with an assortment of tubes and winging materials; to Alan Bramley of Partridge who very kindly gave me a wide selection of hooks to carry out hooking experiments; and to David Adams of Leeda, Paul Burgess of Airflo, and Michael Evans who generously furnished me with a variety of fly lines to play with!

Thanks and appreciation to Mark Bowler and Crawford Little, editors of *Fly Fishing and Fly Tying* and *Salmon Trout & Sea-trout* for giving me permission to reproduce some small sections of text in this book which first appeared in article form in their respective magazines.

Finally, sincere thanks to Jock Woods, ghillie on the Doonfoot fishings.

INTRODUCTION

Forty to fifty years ago, rivers such as the Dee, Spey and Tweed were experiencing excellent runs of spring salmon. Today, the number of spring salmon running in these as well as in many other rivers has reduced drastically, with the main runs now occurring during the summer and autumn. Since the mid-1950s the Tweed has shifted from being a spring fishery to an autumn one – although having said this, the spring run of fish that entered the Tweed during 1995 was reported as being one of the best in twenty years. Why salmon are now running rivers later in the year is open to much debate: some authorities argue that this drastic change is due to the weather patterns which favour the autumn fish; others maintain that the lack of spring fish in our rivers is because of the indiscriminate drift netting practised in that season. I have also heard it said that it could be due to some heredity problem!

It used to be thought that 'like' would breed 'like', but scientific research has shown that this does not seem to be the case regarding spring salmon. A set of statistics I read in an article not so long ago showed that two sea-winter fish only produced about 13 per cent of the returning spring stock, the remaining 87 per cent being grilse. Having said this, in the tests carried out, grilse produced over 98 per cent grilse, and the grilse percentage figures given in the article appear to support the hypothesis that 'like' breeds 'like'. However, the 13 per cent given for the two sea-winter spring fish does nothing to help explain why these fish are disappearing.

Another reason I have heard put forward for the decline of spring salmon is environmentally based, the result of changing river systems, marine water temperatures and so on. But having given the subject a great deal of thought, I am inclined to believe that no one specific element is responsible, and that all of these conjectures carry some degree of explanation. Nevertheless, there are still far too many questions which need to be answered before we can start to make good the lack of these wonderful fish. In order to try and establish the spring run again on many rivers, artificial breeding programmes were introduced and established – although in the main these have proved disappointing, and have not brought about the desired results. It may be that by tampering with the natural selection process we are doing more damage than good.

EXPLAINING THE AUTUMN-RUNNING FISH

I am convinced that the large autumn runs of salmon our rivers are now experiencing is nothing other than a 'bastard' run, my argument being that many of the fish caught during September and early October are not 'autumn' fish at all, but spring and summer salmon which are running later. Anglers on the banks of more than one river have noticed that the fish seem to be 'colouring up' earlier than they used to, and it is certainly true that many of the fish we catch during the early autumn are now very coloured; however, it must be said that most of them are not authentic autumn salmon. And although several anglers accept these salmon as 'autumn' fish, I believe that many of them are in fact late-running springers, summer salmon and grilse. Real autumn fish running our rivers at this time are not red or black, they are silver and firm of flesh, and do not usually don their breeding livery until the waters cool down much later in the season, in mid- to late November. Indeed there is one variety, known locally as 'greybacks' and which run a few of the Ayrshire and Solway rivers, which will run upstream during October and November on one spate, spawn, and then return to the sea on the next, sometimes as silver as the day they migrated as smolts.

From what I have observed, spring salmon, grilse and summer fish still arrive off their respective river mouths at the expected time each year, but then many of them seem to prefer to await the first rains of the summer and autumn equinoxes before ascending. Sometimes this is due to a lack of rain earlier in the year, although I have to admit that this is not always the case; for instance, sometimes following a spate, the expected runs for which anglers have waited patiently do not materialize, with the fish staying out in the coastal waters. Further, I know a number of rivers which used to receive a small run of spring fish, but although these rivers accrue their stocks of fish along the local coasts and in their estuaries at the same time as they did before, these fish do not ascend at the time they did previously, even when water heights and temperatures allow; they now prefer to wait until much later in the year before entering the river.

Prior to the UDN of the 1960s, the spring fish which used to ascend the rivers I am talking about took the first opportunity they got to run upstream. Now, however, those few remaining spring fish which still arrive off the river mouths early in the year refuse to run, regardless of water height and temperature, and await instead the arrival of the summer and autumn spates. Generally when these spring and summer fish ran the rivers during their accustomed times, the majority had long since ascended to the upper beats come the autumn. Yet today in many rivers it is not uncommon for stale, coloured spring fish, adorned with sea-lice, to be taken in the lower and middle beats during July and August, when forty to fifty years ago stale, coloured fish with sea-lice at this time were almost unheard of. Now admittedly I wasn't even born then, let alone fishing, but I do have a tongue in my head and I used it to ask those who were. And although back in the late 1960s through to the late 1970s, (when I *was* fishing) I remember coloured 'autumn' fish, I don't remember them being so numerous as they have been of late. Even so, my own view is still that 'autumn' salmon have not increased in numbers as some would have us believe, but that these larger runs of fish are in fact that of a bastard run brought about by a number of factors.

THE 'FLY-ONLY' RULE

Today, many riparian owners and district boards have introduced, or are trying to introduce, 'fly-only' rules to their fisheries in order to try and conserve salmon stocks. For example, the River Dee District Salmon Fishery Board was one which introduced a 'fly-only' rule prior to the opening of the 1995 season, along with a number of proposals implemented to try and save their dwindling stocks after the Whitley fish counter recorded dangerously low numbers of returning adult springers. As it turned out, the counter was later found to be faulty and so the introduction of the new 'rules' caused a great deal of controversy. Nevertheless, there are many rivers where 'fly-only' is the rule during the first and last few weeks of the season, the Tweed being the best known. So why *do* the district boards and riparian owners on these rivers impose this rule during these times? In the opening weeks of the season it is to facilitate the unhooking and safe return of kelts, while in the late season it is to help reduce the numbers of stale, gravid fish being killed. A salmon 'gut'-hooked on a worm is very difficult if not impossible to unhook, and as a result has to be killed. Now some will consider this to be rubbish, but I have seen real experts misjudge the situation – they give the fish too much line and end up hooking it after it has swallowed the worms. Although I have never heard of salmon swallowing a spinning lure, they do, however, often become very firmly impaled, and as a result are kept out of the water when landed for an over-long period of time, unlike the majority of fish taken on the fly. This is because the hooks on a spinning lure are often pulled in well beyond the barbs by anglers who strike hard on feeling the take.

Another reason for banning spinning at this time of the year is that many of the lures used by anglers employ two or more sets of treble hooks. The damage caused by one deeply embedded hook can be bad enough, let alone two or three. In addition to this, salmon generally have a tendency to take a spinning lure with much greater force than they do a fly. Yes, I know there are times when fish will take a fly fiercely, especially cock fish later in the season when they become aggressive – but on the whole, salmon will take a fly much more gently than they do a spinning lure. In the spring I have seen salmon hooked in the back of the throat on long-winged flies such as the Collie Dog, but in all my experience I have never seen a salmon that has actually swallowed one. Having said that, although salmon are usually easier to free from a 'fly', they can and still do become firmly impaled, especially if a treble or double hook is employed. Perhaps a better solution would be to encourage anglers to use barbless hooks. Across the Atlantic barbless singles have been the accepted practice for many years; in fact, in many States it is illegal to use anything else. If anglers in the UK were obliged to use single barbless hooks there would be an outcry. Perhaps a compromise situation could be implemented, so that doubles and trebles could be used *provided* they were de-barbed. I am sure this would be much more palatable.

CONSERVING SALMON STOCKS

Not only should we be taking steps to conserve spring salmon numbers, we should also be striving to preserve all salmon stocks. Come September and October, fish start to become stale and coloured, their flesh dry and grey. These fish are no longer edible, and if caught, they should be returned to the river. Some riparian owners have strict policies regarding the returning of fish. Some insist that after a certain date, all hen fish regardless of their condition should be returned, and that only the freshest of cock fish are killed. I for one would have no complaint against this. I would, however, criticize owners who take bookings and do not specify or make clear in their booking documentation their policy regarding the returning of fish; I have experienced the situation myself where the owner did not state in writing, or make it clear to guests, that he wished all fish caught to be returned. One owner would pressurize the anglers he saw catching fish almost aggressively, instructing them to return the fish regardless of their condition. He did this to me on one occasion. As it happened, as soon as I saw the fish I knew I would return it – but the same owner also asked to see a fish my wife had killed and put in the

Two fresh-run autumn fish from the River Doon.

freezer. This was blatantly questioning our judgement, and is an attitude which I find quite sickening. Let me assure you the fish was silver, fresh run, bearing sea-lice and perfectly clean.

I believe we must all play a part in trying to conserve salmon stocks, but in my opinion the fate of any fish – unless caught by a novice who might not recognize a fish which should be returned, or unless the return of fish has been expressed and accepted as part of the conditions of the let – should be determined by the angler and not the owner. Returning autumn fish which are not suitable for the table is the correct thing to do, but we should not go game fishing with the intention of returning everything we catch: this would change what is a sport into a game from which one derives personal pleasure. When I go fishing my intention is to kill what I catch, and if it is not suitable for eating then it is returned to get on with Nature's business. I feel if the owner mentioned above did not want any fish killed, then he should not strictly have been leasing his fishing.

THE SUCCESSFUL SALMON FLY FISHER

It has long been my ambition to write an integrative book on salmon fly fishing. Before I even began I spent a long time trying to identify the areas that I considered would be of the most benefit and interest to the salmon fly fisher who wants to graduate beyond the 'occasional fish'. In order to address these anglers I decided not to provide answers to the sort of questions which arise so commonly in the angling press, since the subject matter in many of the topics does little to exercise and broaden the minds of those salmon fly fishers who *think*.

I have often been asked what makes one salmon fly fisherman more successful than others, and to this I usually reply that it is not so much what you see him doing that makes the difference, but the little things you don't. Some things you cannot and will not see, because he will be doing them within the confines of his home or tackle shop. At home he will be taking care to record the day's events in his fishing register. He will have spent time sorting out and discarding the old and rusting hooks from his fly boxes; a rusty hook will not take the burden of either a lively or a heavy fish for long. And in the tackle shop he will be taking care to select only the 'best' hooks and lines and so on.

On the river bank the differences between the successful fisherman and the not-so-successful angler will be subtle and difficult to spot. It might be that when his/her fly prepares to swing out of the fast current on the far side of the pool he gives a small upstream mend to keep it lingering there for a few seconds longer. Perhaps, on the other hand, he will accelerate its exit from the faster water by putting in a downstream mend, a small one for a slight increase in speed and a larger one for a significant increase. He may also try pulling in line, a few inches to simulate a small creature moving unhurriedly forward in the flow, or a few feet quickly to emulate the panic bolting action of a frightened fish. And if no one is waiting to fish down the pool behind him, he may try them all. This is not because he is chancing his luck or hogging the best spot, it is because he knows that a change of fly speed or direction will often provoke a fish into taking a fly which it has previously refused. On other occasions, depending on the colour and height of water, he may try a different size or style of fly.

If the above ruses do not work he may decide to cover the water with a fly that has a wing made from a material which gives superior mobility to that previously used, or he may simply change to a fly with more presence. Or he might try changing to a fly tied on either a heavier or lighter hook in order to alter the depth of presentation. Another possible reason for his success is that he may be casting a longer line and bringing his fly through the only stretch of water that holds fish. It may also be that his leader is turning over properly, resulting in the fly starting to fish the instant it enters the water, instead of sinking corpse-like until the current straightens out the leader and brings the fly to life. And if he takes a fish on a tube or a Waddington after others have fished a similar fly through the same water, it could be because his fly has a different sized treble than that used by the other anglers. An oversize hook will make either of these popular fly types swim tail heavy and tail down. Let me assure you, a tail-heavy fly will do nothing to encourage fish to take hold of it.

Looking back through the realms of angling history, the great names – men such as Drury, Ryghini, Waddington and Wood – were all innovators, not conformists. Most of all, though, they were anglers who used their brains. I hope that in this book I will help anglers to develop a more thinking, investigative, positive approach to their own fishing, that the information provided will facilitate meaningful learning. Even so, trying to tell someone how to catch fish is a bit like a top darts player trying to show you how he scores treble top: he will show you how he does it, but when it comes to your turn it's a different story! Thus, practice may perfect the angler's hand/eye/motor-neurone co-ordination and help him cast a fly line thirty yards, or place a spinning lure or bait to within an inch of where he would like it to go, but there is no substitute for experience, and this can only be gained by actually fishing. Having said that, some people can spend a lifetime fishing and never hook a salmon; others have hooked fish on their first cast. In short, there really is no justice; but if you want the maximum pleasure from the sport, be patient, because the more difficult the trade, the longer is the apprenticeship.

The whole object when fishing for salmon, whether with a fly or a spinning lure, is to present it in such a fashion that it will provoke a fish into opening its mouth and taking hold. Fly fishing is one method of presenting a lure to fish, yet there exists some of the richest literature in the world about it; in fact, the only other angling subject matter I know of that boasts equal literary output is dry fly fishing for trout in the chalk streams of the south of England. However, even though fly fishing is just one way of seducing the noble salmon, it is the one branch of the sport which is open to all sorts of fallacies. Some 'fly-only' anglers restrict themselves to this method simply because it gives them the most pleasure. Others, however, assume an uncalled-for, self-appointed snobbish attitude towards anything other than fly, that has nothing to do with maximizing their pleasure: it is about image, status, and how they will be perceived. If you don't believe me, take a

Arndilly on the Spey.

walk along a famous beat on one of the major classics during a prime week.

MY OWN PREFERENCES

Personally speaking, I derive more pleasure from taking a fish on fly than by any other means. It is not that I believe it to be better or more sporting than the other methods, because it is not: all legal methods are sporting. However, as far as I am concerned it is one that requires superior rivercraft skills and presentation knowledge, that is to say, increased understanding of how various current nuances and speeds will precipitate the travel of the fly line across pools, and subsequently how this will affect the fly's behaviour through the fish-holding sections. In addition to this, it requires greater motor-neurone co-ordination than any of the others. I get immense personal pleasure from Spey-casting a long line and seeing the backing splice go through the top ring. I like the feeling of a long, double-handed rod bending and bucking under the weight of a fish. I also enjoy the music of the fly reel when a fish runs: to my ears there is no tune like it.

This is not to say that I don't like fishing with a spinning rod. In my first book *Salmon Fishing in River and Stream* I discuss at length many spinning techniques that I have employed with success over the years. Where the situation or the terrain makes fly fishing impossible and a different approach necessary, I will use a spinning rod. Although I prefer using the fly, I do enjoy trying to catch running fish in small, heavily wooded streams during spate conditions. I particularly like fishing difficult places, the sort of spots most

A visiting angler fishing the Aberlour Angling Association water on the Spey.

anglers will walk past. These places generally have very little space in which to cast a lure properly; more often than not there will only be a small gap to put the tip of your rod through. Casting in the conventional fashion is out of the question, whilst flicking a lure through a small opening into any likely looking spots is not for the faint-hearted. This method of spinning for salmon demands a high level of skill which generally separates the real anglers from the posers since it requires great rivercraft and casting skill. Moreover this type of fishing is not for the immaculately clad brigade who like the 'going' to be good: these river bank 'jungles' are unsympathetic places, and anglers, tackle and clothing usually pay the price. However, the rewards from fishing these places are often worth the hardships. I do not consider that taking a fish on spinner is any less of an achievement, or less sporting than taking one on fly; after all, a salmon on the bank is a salmon on the bank. Nevertheless, in saying this, for the past three years I have not needed to use my spinning tackle, as most of my fishing has been done on larger rivers that enjoy open water. One interesting thing I have noticed, though, is that my catches do not appear to have dwindled at all – if anything it is the reverse.

Another reason I prefer the fly rod to the spinner is that I find it more relaxing; it also allows you to keep more on the move, because all you really need apart from the rod and reel is a box of suitably sized flies and a spool of nylon, and perhaps a priest and a thermometer. All of these can quite easily be carried in the front pocket of my chest waders or wading jacket, or my waistcoat if I happen to be wearing one. I do not like burdening myself with scores of fly boxes, or other items of tackle which may never be used. A day's fishing whilst heavily laden down does not help anyone to concentrate on the task at hand, that of catching fish, and those who set out in this manner seldom become successful anglers because more often than not they do not maximize their chances of a fish. Generally these anglers will leave their tackle bags at the head of a pool before commencing to fish it down. Then usually after the first two or three pools, they will start to restrict their fishing to just a small stretch of water because they get tired walking back to the head of every pool they have fished before going on downstream to the next one. Not only does this waste their valuable fishing time, it is also very tedious – and further, once an angler becomes tired, he/she will usually get fed up very quickly and as a result will not execute his skills to the best of his ability.

I remember a week's fishing a few years back on a Solway river when my wife and I were sharing a beat with two other rods, a gentleman and his young lady friend. They were both laden down with large, bulging rucksacks that would not have been out of place on the back of a Sherpa going forth on an Everest expedition. Some anglers might have assumed that they were inexperienced, and so had brought everything along in order to be prepared for any eventuality. However, after watching them and speaking to them, I soon came to the conclusion that they were really no more than 'posers'. My wife and I saw them fishing on only two other occasions during the remainder of the week – perhaps because they were worn out from humping their rucksacks about!

1 FOR THE RECORD

Many anglers either cannot be bothered, or do not want to keep a record of the fish they catch. Some simply consider it too much trouble, others perhaps who do keep a catch record, document only the date, and the weight. Although this is better than nothing, all it really achieves is a fish tally, and in following such practices these anglers deny themselves an invaluable source of reference material. It might be argued that there is no need to take detailed notes of a day's success, but this must surely be a mistake: the salmon is such a fickle creature to tempt that any knowledge gained through the successful hooking of one should not be left just to memory, but the details of the experience documented. True, everyone remembers their first salmon as if it was yesterday; but who can recall the exact details of water height and clarity, the overhead conditions, or the fly size and pattern that took a fish some fifteen years past? I agree that if it happened to be a fish of a lifetime everything will be quite vivid; but what if it chanced to be a small one of 6 or 7lb? Is the knowledge gained from the hooking of small salmon of no significance? As far as salmon fishing is concerned there is no better knowledge gained than that achieved through personal experience, and what a waste to lose all these details just because you can't be bothered to write them down.

Date & Place	Conditions	Catch	Reflections

Fig 1 A bad example of a catch register sheet.

To my mind, the fishing registers commonly available in tackle shops are far from adequate, and although appearing to contain all the necessary divisions, are really far too basic. I very much doubt if such a catch return sheet as shown in Fig 1 was conceived by an angler, let alone a serious salmon fisher. This one *could* be used to include additional information relating to a catch, but as so often happens when something becomes a compromise and is simply adapted, it could very quickly turn into no more than a collection of scribbles. This would not make for the quick and easy extraction of any desired information because any data that was added in would very quickly become randomized and scattered within the modified columns. If the insertion and extraction of information cannot be done easily, then the whole object of the exercise is lost.

Thus a catch record sheet of the format as shown in Fig 1 would not be an effectual or a helpful register. The catch register sheet which I designed to meet all my own particular requirements contains eleven main sections, five of which are subdivided further; in this format I can extract information for any specific event at a glance (*see* Fig 2).

RECORDING THE DATE

The first column down the left hand side is for the date. This might not seem an important item to register, but in recording it we then know when during the season the fish was caught, and can then cross-correlate the other associated particulars of the catch to see if there was anything unusual about it: for example, whether or not the fish was taken on a large fly when the air and water temperatures dictated a small one. In order to emphasize this and certain other points, I have tabulated some results from the 1993 and 1994 seasons that do not correspond to the expected. Thus the first fish on the sheet came from the Little Stream on the Strathspey Angling Improvement Association water of the Spey a few miles upstream of Grantown. At first one might think that there is nothing unusual about this catch, but what it shows is that with even a 3in (76mm) rise, Spey salmon are still willing to take a relatively small fly (the fish taking a size 8 Silver Stoat).

In my opinion a great many anglers who fish the Spey for the first time are inclined to use too large a fly. On the day in question I witnessed anglers fishing flies larger than 1½in (38mm). To add further to my argument that Spey fish will take small flies even when the river is flowing with additional height I have included the details of a fish I took on 11.7.94: it took a size 10 Silver Stoat's Tail when the water was running with 3in (76mm) on the gauge.

Some anglers may contend that I cannot come to this kind of conclusion from two fish: true, I cannot, but I have not based my whole opinion on these two. Thus if you look at the four days on the Doon dated from the 28.7.93 to 4.8.93 you will notice that all the salmon taken by myself on these dates were on large flies, even although the water was only a few inches above normal. If you look at the difference between the air and water temperatures for these dates you will see that there was approximately a 6°F difference in favour of the air. Under normal circumstances I would have employed a much smaller fly, but during the dates

Date	River	Pool	Temp		Water Height			Water Clarity			Overhead			Lure Details	Salmon		Weight		Time Caught
			W	A	H	N	L	T	Clr	C	D	S	M		♂	♀	lbs	ozs	
19.7.93	Spey	Little Stream	58	66	+3					×			×	Size 8 Silver Stoat		×	5	2	3.00p.m.
28.7.93	Doon	Polnessan	59	64	+5				×				×	Size 6 Ally's Shrimp		×	7	0	4.15p.m.
29.7.93	Doon	Kiln	56	60	+6				×				×	2" Waddington Ally's Shrimp		×	/	/	3.15p.m.
3.8.93	Doon	Old Brig	57	60	+6				×		×			2" Waddington Ally's Shrimp	×		/	/	9.30a.m.
4.8.93	Doon	Salmon Lies	57	62	+4					×		×		Size 6 Ally's Shrimp	×		7	4	10.00a.m.
7.8.93	Stinchar	Grey Stanes	55	60	+18			×					×	2" Orange Tube Fly		×	6	8	11.00a.m.
12.8.93	Doon	Clach	55	61	+3				×				×	2" Waddington Ally's Shrimp		×	/		3.30p.m.
20.10.93	Bladnoch	Market	44	49			-2			×		×		Size 6 Ally's Shrimp	×		6	0	11.15a.m.
13.11.93	Irvine	Grannies	50	56	+12				×				×	2" Orange Tube Fly		×	4	8	4.14p.m.
														1994					
8.7.94	Spey	Clach Na Strone	56	64	+6					×	×			Size 6 Orange & Yellow Haiwing		×	7	2	7.30p.m.
11.7.94	Spey	Polnacour	57	66	+3					×			×	Size 10 Silver Stoats Tail		×	7	3	11.50p.m.
5.8.94	Stinchar	Craig Run	55	63	+12				×				×	Size 6 Claret & Orange Fly	×		9	3	12.00 noon
31.10.94	Doon	Pump House	53	59	+7			×			×			2" Waddington Jungle Buck	×		14	4	11.50a.m.

Fig 2 Salmon catch samples for 1993–94.

Temp.: W = Water, A = Air. **Water Height:** H = High, L = Low, N = Normal. **Water Clarity:** T = Turbid, Clr = Clearing, C = Clear.
Overhead: D = Dull, S = Sunny, M = Mixture.

shown, overnight rain was causing the river level to fluctuate up and down like a yo-yo, even though the gauge in the morning was reading between +4 and +6in (10 and 15mm). Other rods fishing at the same time who employed small flies did not fair so well. In short, I have found that a large fly, rather than a small one, brings more fish to the bank when the water height is constantly fluctuating and as a result keeping the fish unsettled.

Finally, if you take a look at the details of the fish I took on the 20.10.93 from the Bladnoch you will see that the fish took a size 6 Ally's Shrimp when the water was 2in (50mm) below its normal level. The fly in question was almost 3in (76mm). This fish overturned all of my previously accepted knowledge, because normally when fishing under similar conditions I would have employed only tiny flies. What this particular occurrence once again brought home to me was that just when you think you have got these creatures figured out, they wipe out everything that you previously thought you knew about them.

RECORDING THE RIVER AND THE POOL

The second and third columns name the river and pool. Since no two rivers fish the same under similar conditions I find this invaluable reference material, especially when fishing a number of different rivers and beats throughout the season. If I have fished the river before, I can see at a glance which particular section of the beat, or which pools fished best for the prevailing conditions, i.e. the high- and low-water pools.

RECORDING TEMPERATURE

The next column I have subdivided into two, one for the water (W), the other for air (A) temperature. For whatever reason a salmon rises to a fly or to any other lure, I have come to believe that one of the foremost factors determining its taking behaviour is the temperature differential between the air and the water.

RECORDING WATER HEIGHT

I have always regarded water height as being *the* crucial element for success when fishing for salmon. This section of the record sheet I have divided into three: H = High, N = Normal, and L= Low. In these I simply enter + inches, 0, or − inches, depending on the prevailing height at the time. Every river has its own productive height, and by keeping a record of water heights when I have had success I can see which river will fish best at any given time. This is particularly useful if I can choose between more than one venue: why fish one river at an unproductive height when another could offer a better chance of a fish? For example, I live within an hour's drive of the Doon and the Stinchar. Although both have different catchment areas given general widespread rain, both rivers will see a rise in water. I have found from fishing both rivers regularly that the Stinchar fishes very well with a +18in (45cm) rise, while the Doon does not. On spate rivers such as these, this type of information is of prime interest.

On classic rivers where fish can run upstream without an increase in water height, it would appear (from my records) that the majority of the fish I have been lucky enough to tempt seemed to favour coming to my fly once the river had dropped back and started to run again at normal height. Whereas rivers which depend on rain to allow fish access generally provide the best sport when they achieve a particular height and colour.

RECORDING WATER CLARITY

Water clarity can make a difference, not because the fish cannot see the lure being offered, but because of the suspended matter: a river carrying a lot of suspended matter, or running black due to an increase in peat juice, can put the fish 'off' the take. Very often a noticeable change in colour brought about by a reduction in suspended substance, whether it be from mud or peat juice, can make all the difference. These columns are labelled T = Turbid, Clr = Clearing, C = Clear (Normal). The relevant column is simply marked with an X.

RECORDING OVERHEAD CONDITIONS

Next I identify the overhead conditions present at the time, and in this section I have three: D = Dull, S = Sunny, and M = Mixed. According to the thirteen catches indexed on the specimen sheet in Fig 2 you will see that 'Mixed' overhead conditions were best. In saying this, however, in looking through my other catch sheets, 'Dull' and 'Mixed' overhead conditions are, in fact much on a par with each other, while 'Sunny' conditions are by far the worst.

RECORDING LURE DETAILS

This column lists the lure sizes on which I have caught the fish. Some anglers when initially selecting a fly place great emphasis on its pattern or colour; my own preference is to determine the correct size for the prevailing conditions at the time, and this to me is of more significance than the colour or dressing. As you can see from Fig 2, the majority of fish indexed in the examples given have been killed on either a predominantly orange, or black fly. This is not because I think that these are the only colours that will kill fish, they are simply the two colours I prefer to use. By fishing these two colours in suitable sizes I am fishing with confidence and in the knowledge that they have caught me fish before – which is half the battle when fishing for salmon. Personally I see no point in continually changing one colour of fly for another. If I had given examples of fish taken on spinning lures you would have noticed that the majority of fish I hooked were on a Devon minnow. As with flies, I rarely use anything other than two, a Yellow Belly, or a Black and Red. One interesting factor that comes to light after checking my records is that 75 per cent of all hen fish taken fell to the Yellow Belly, while 68 per cent of all cock fish fell to the Black and Red – though I am bound to say that I have no conclusive proof that each sex has a colour preference.

RECORDING THE SEX OF FISH TAKEN

If nothing else, this tells me the ratio of cock to hen fish caught. One other interesting characteristic that I have noted is that as the season progresses, cock fish seem more willing to move to a large lure, rather than a small one, particularly from the end of September onwards. As well as this, it would appear from my catch register that some pools seem to produce mostly hen fish, while others give up mainly cocks. Why this is so I am at a loss to explain. The column that deals with the weight of fish caught might not seem very important, but by paying attention to the weight and pool statistics it allows us to fish specific pools, or lies that have produced the 'better' fish in the past. Perhaps this is mere coincidence. On many occasions however, over the years, I have taken double-figure fish from the same place within a pool under similar conditions,

Most autumn fish which are carefully returned to the river will, if not caught again by some 'fishmonger', find their way onto the redds.

that is as regards water height, temperature, and clarity. I am not alone in believing that certain lies attract big fish, while others are only tenanted by smaller fish, for example grilse: other angling authors in their books have also propounded this observation, and there is no getting away from the fact that certain lies only attract the larger fish.

RECORDING THE TIME

The next section of the sheet records the time a fish is hooked, and by analysing this information over a certain period it soon became apparent – to me, anyway – that certain patterns appear. On larger river systems where fish can run without an increase in water height there are times when it pays to fish even when the water is low: although they will not be running in numbers, a few will still be nosing their way upstream and knowing when these fish enter your beat can help reduce the chance of a blank.

The time taken for fish to arrive in a beat is of particular interest to those anglers who fish the smaller spate streams. If the catch times are looked at in conjunction with a high tide time-table, it very soon becomes apparent that the fish running each river system appear in the respective stretches at specific times. By knowing when a run of fresh fish is likely to appear in the beat you are fishing, you can spare yourself a lot of wasted time and concentrate your efforts at a period when you are most likely to be rewarded. The best taking times cannot be identified for the rivers listed in Fig 2, but let me assure you I have enough information tabulated in my catch book to convince me that there is a unequivocal pattern regarding the time fish arrive in a number of the beats on these rivers.

RECORDING MISSED FISH

As a final point I would also recommend you take note of any fish that happen to come off. Some of those anglers who keep records do not include these salmon, and this I feel is a mistake. I am not saying that they should record plucks, tweaks or pulls, as these may not in fact be salmon; but if a fish has been lost at the net or while being played it should, to my mind, become part of your statistics. The information gained from a lost fish is just as valuable as that earned from one that has been killed, or returned. In the sample of salmon caught in Fig 2, lost and returned fish are recognized among my own statistics by a diagonal line through the 'lb oz' column.

2 FLY COLOUR, SIZE AND SPEED

There is absolutely no doubt in my mind that water temperature plays a significant factor in the migratory as well as the taking behaviour of adult salmon, So before we look at the age-old contentious issue of fly selection, I think it best if we first take a look at this. Since the salmon is primarily a cold-blooded animal, it will take on the temperature of its surroundings, i.e. that of the water, and this will therefore affect its metabolic and respiratory systems. If the metabolic and respiratory rate is low, the fish will be lethargic and incapable of moving far or fast, and this is the main reason why spring salmon seldom show themselves; it is also why the salmon that enter the rivers in January or February are apparently reluctant to run far upstream. At this time of the year – mid-winter – the sea is often very much warmer than the river into which they are entering. Even during the middle of winter the sea temperatures around the coast of the UK very seldom drop below 45°F (7.2°C). During January and February the water temperatures of rivers may very well be in the lower 30°F (0–1°C) and although salmon have been recorded entering rivers with such water temperatures, they prefer to wait until the water has risen to the mid 40s°F (6–8°C). Furthermore, when they enter the river, how far they travel upstream is generally determined by

'temperature' barriers, very often a weir, or a set of falls which they will refuse to negotiate until the water temperature rises above the mid 40s°F.

The crucial temperature at which they will negotiate such barriers appears to vary from one river to another. Fish in some river systems have been known to arrive below an obstacle when the water temperature has been high enough for them to ascend, but instead of doing so they stick around, refusing to go any further until the air temperature rises, even if the river is flowing at an ideal height to allow them to ascend further. Derek Knowles in his book *Salmon on a Dry Fly* wrote the following concerning a set of falls that formed a temperature barrier in Sutherland:

> One year I spent three consecutive days watching this fall when the water was right for the fish to run. At 4.00 p.m. on the third day the sun, which had shone from lunch time, lifted the water temperature from 46°F to just over 52°F, and at 4.30 p.m. the fish which had been milling around the pool for three days started to run the falls. The following year the fish arrived at the foot of the main falls when the temperature reached 48°F but the weather was not kind. For over a week it was cold and overcast and the water temperature varied only

between 46°F and 50°F and the salmon waited below the falls. The water was perfect for the fish to run with frequent little freshets, but the sun remained hidden. It was ten days before the sun broke through, the temperature rose and the fish went over the falls.

As well as this, albeit to a somewhat lesser extent, the air temperature can determine their progress, with salmon refusing to negotiate obstacles when the water and air temperatures are very close to each other.

FLY COLOUR

Can salmon detect colour? I believe they can. Fresh-run fish straight from the sea seem partial to a brightly coloured fly, therefore when fishing at a time when there is likely to be an influx of new fish my own preference is to use an orange fly such as an Ally's Shrimp, or a fly of my own tying called Keachie's Krill. Most salmon when they return to the river of their birth treat anglers' flies with the utmost contempt. Since the total number of fish that get caught represents only a very small percentage of the overall body entering a river, we must therefore try to maximize our chances of stimulating a response from the few that are willing to take. I believe that the majority of fresh fish which take an angler's fly – or any other lure for that matter – and get caught, do so because their feeding memory has not been fully suppressed. Therefore when there is a chance of a fresh fish I like to use something which will hopefully bring about a response and so I fish with a fly that represents a creature on which the salmon fed at sea.

At sea salmon are ravenous feeders and as a result quickly increase in size and bulk. Their gluttonous feeding behaviour does not therefore allow for them to be particularly selective in what they choose to eat. Known food items taken by salmon at sea are capelin, herring fry, krill (a collective name given to shrimp-like crustaceans of the *Parathemisto* and *Eusirus* genera, and Euphausiid of the *Meganyctiphanes* genus of prawns, and sand eels. I personally don't believe that they consciously seek out these items; as far as a salmon is concerned, if it looks edible it probably is, and as a result it will prey upon anything which looks likely to provide it with nourishment. So when fishing for fresh-run fish I tend to use flies that resemble one of the previously listed creatures, particularly those that have a shrimpy, crustacean-like appearance.

My overall intention is not just to show these fresh fish something that looks shrimpy in shape, I also like to reproduce the essential coloration found in many of these creatures. A few years back I started to think about the colours found on the more popular shrimp patterns. The majority of the better known ones have either a two-colour body of red/black, or orange/black floss, or a uniform body of silver ribbed with an oval or flat tinsel; but although most of them catch fish, one pattern looks very much like another – in other words, they are somewhat restricted in conveying their pretence. After giving it much thought I came to realise that what most of them lacked was the correct body colour, that is, a greeny, iridescent sparkle. Now, those anglers who think this is not a sensible colour for such a fly are wrong, because the salinity of the sea distorts and reflects light differently from that transmitted through fresh water, and light reflected off a shiny or silvery surface appears to take on an iridescent, greeny hue. If you have ever fished for mackerel and seen them twisting and turning as they near the surface you will know what I mean; and if you have sat by a rock pool after the tide has turned and it contains shrimps you will have witnessed the same green dancing iridescent sheen as the sun bounces off their watery flanks as they dart about.

I therefore decided to tie up a pattern which would reproduce this greeny iridescence when it was fished in freshwater. As well as this I wanted to incorporate the colours orange and red into the fly because so many of the established shrimp and prawn patterns have one or both of these colours; I also thought red would help simulate the haemoglobin which can sometimes be seen pulsing through shrimps' bodies, and the red mottling sometimes found along their backs. As for orange, this I hoped would simulate the coloration of the *Parathemisto* and *Eusirus* shrimps, known food items of salmon, the orangey tinge brought on by the parasite *Parandinium*. (The dressing for Keachie's Krill is included in *Appendix II*.)

The Salmon's Visual Response
Published scientific research on the optical response of fish has established that the

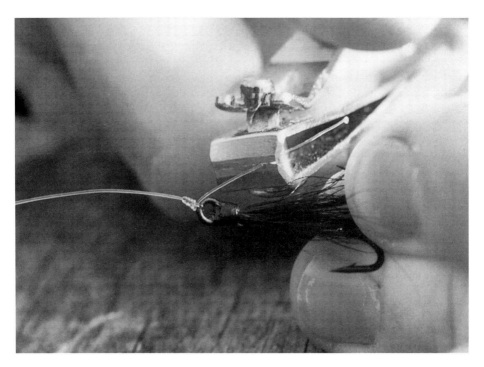

When trimming excess nylon, never cut it right up close to the eye of the fly but always allow ⅛ to ¼in (4 to 6mm). I have never found this tail putting fish off.

salmon's eye contains both rods and cones in its construction, and this means they can distinguish and acknowledge colour. Further, not only can they see colour, they also have diurnal vision: this means the cones are retracted come twilight when scotopic conditions prevail, and then return to normal for photopic conditions. As an animal species evolves it is rational to suppose that its visual response will be specifically engineered to aid its survival. Needless to say the salmon is no exception, and its eyesight is one of the best in the animal kingdom. Its eyes are large for its size, as are the rest of the visual components, the optic nerves and optic tectum constituting more than two-thirds of the overall size of the salmon's brain. With the optic elements being so well developed it is logical to suppose that vision is the salmon's primary sensory means, and that it will use this for hunting.

Colour Sensitivity in Salmon

The three main processes involved regarding vision, are known as the optical, the transduction and the physiological stages. The first, the optical stage, occurs naturally when an image is projected onto the retina. Next is the transduction stage, when the light-sensitive cells absorb photons and generate the necessary electrical signals. The physiological stage happens when the electrical signals are analysed.

For an animal to be colour sensitive it must have a retina with visual pigments. These visual pigments are chromoproteins, with a chromophoric cluster related to vitamin A1 (retinol), or A2 (dehydroretinol) (in Man, the retinol chemicals are derived from beta-carotene). Colour detection therefore depends on the absorptive ability of the cluster colour pigmentations present in a retina, and in order to ascertain those present in the cone cluster we use a process called microspectrophotometry. Tests on a number of different species of fish have shown that there are mainly two cluster colour pigmentations present: rhodopsin (green) and porphyropsin (red). It has been found that the cone clusters in fish which frequent a marine environment have predominantly rhodopsin, or green-based vision, while freshwater fish have more porphyropsin, giving them predominantly red-based vision. Some species, however, frequent both environments, and the salmon is one of these since it migrates from freshwater to salt water and back to freshwater during its breeding migrations.

So what colours *does* the salmon see? Microspectrophotometry tests done on the retinas of Coho salmon during their marine life have shown that the retinas are dominated by rhodopsin (green); but when the fish start to move into brackish water prior to their upstream migration, the colour pigments in the retinas change to porphyropsin (red). On entering freshwater, 90 per cent of the retinas are dominated by porphyropsin, or red visual pigment. Similar tests done on Sockeye salmon show these fish to have a rhodopsin – or green-dominated – retina with only a slight increase in porphyropsin – red – at spawning time.

Initial preliminary microspectrophometric testing of the Atlantic salmon has shown that their retina colour pigmentations closely follow that of the Coho. Some self-appointed authorities have suggested that the salmon's colour detection capability is reduced in relation to the time they spend in freshwater. However, their

Summer on the Spey. Time for small flies and floating line.

notion of progressive 'colour blindness' in salmon is based upon research done on mammals – i.e. animals that have to feed frequently in order to extract the necessary nutrients to sustain their biological and physiological functions – and it is easy to see the one major flaw in this theory when related to salmon: as a result of thousands of years of evolution, fish can now go without food for many months – yet as far

as I see it, Nature is hardly going to allow a reduction in the efficiency of the salmon's primary sensory system.

Now, even supposing salmon *do* suffer a reduction in colour sensitivity when they are in freshwater, I don't believe it would be nearly as severe as certain people would have us believe. My argument is this, if salmon colour detection is comprehensively reduced the longer they are in freshwater, why then do cock salmon undergo such a drastic change in skin pigmentation when they approach spawning time? Based on the 'chemical deficiency theory' – that is, that time spent in freshwater will adversely reduce the salmon's colour pigmentations in the retina – a change of skin colour in cock fish would be a waste of time and energy: surely, if salmon were insensitive to colour after a prolonged stay in freshwater, then Nature would not dictate this colour change?

One angling writer of eminence only recently suggested that even if the salmon's eye could detect colour, its brain might not be able to distinguish differences. On this I do not agree: as far as I am concerned, Nature would not provide an animal with the means of colour detection, and then prohibit the use of that faculty. However, another conjecture suggested to me by an academic working in the Optometry Department of the Caledonian University of Glasgow while researching the subject matter was more interesting, and has certainly given me food for thought: when I mentioned the colour change in the livery of cock salmon at spawning time, he suggested that even though this change does take place, it doesn't necessarily establish colour dominance. He proposed it could well be the patternation of the different skin colours which are the expressing factor, and not the pigmentations themselves.

At the end of all this conjecture, we will never know in actual fact if a lure having a high visibility factor as opposed to an all-black one will make any difference to a salmon in its determination as to whether to take or not. I know that there have been recorded instances of fish apparently refusing a fly of one colour, and then rising and taking one of another. Now, if the fly was presented by two different anglers, then it could be argued that the fly was presented in a slightly different fashion and that the change in presentation stimulated the fish into taking. Generally, though, when an angler changes his fly, his second choice is often presented in precisely the same fashion as the one he has just replaced, and I believe that generally what occurs at these times is that the salmon, for one reason or another, suddenly comes 'on the take' and as a result would possibly have risen to the original fly if presented with it again. Therefore these instances of fish taking one colour and refusing another prove nothing.

THE ATTRACTIONS OF THE 'WILLIE GUNN'

A few years back I was commissioned by an editor of a magazine to write an article on the origins of the famous Willie Gunn salmon fly. I discovered that the original fly was intended for spring fish and had the yellow, orange and black tied in stacked fashion. However, over the years since its inception, autumn anglers fishing the Brora have discovered that late-running fish coming into the river seem to prefer the fly with the yellow, orange and black hair well mixed. Having given this difference in tying preferences some thought, I have come up with a possible explanation for this: the original spring version of the Willie Gunn is generally a much more gaudy affair, with the yellow and orange bunches of hair lying stacked on top of each other. These flies are tied on stainless steel Brora shanks and as a result are quite hefty beasts; they are also fished in conjunction with a relatively fast sinking line. Taking these points into account, it is reasonable to suppose that most of these flies will be working at eye level to the fish. Any light penetrating the water will therefore be partially diffused due to the filtering action of any suspended sediment or natural water tint present at the time. When this occurs, most of the light from the visible end of the spectrum will be removed, and any incident light present after filtration and absorption takes place will tend to be towards the yellow and orange end of the spectrum. The yellows and the oranges in the fly will therefore be greatly increased. Reflected light from the river bed at this time will also help to highlight the fly's presence.

Later in the year the situation is different, however, because during the autumn the mixed wing version of the fly is mostly tied on long-shanked trebles or doubles, and it is fished higher in the water. Salmon will therefore be viewing the fly from beneath, and not nose to nose, and any light now passing through these flies will not be filtered to the same extent as that passing through the deeper-fished spring fly. The fly will therefore take on a much more tenuous presence, and any highlighting of the yellow and orange will be kept to a minimum due to the superior translucency of the dyed hair. Nor will reflected light from the river bed play any part in highlighting the coloured hair of the autumn flies being fished higher in the water, because any light present will be so attenuated by the time it reaches the fly that it will not be capable of providing any worthwhile illumination from below. At the same time the denser black hairs will restrict any light from passing through them and will be appearing in silhouette. These blacker, denser hairs will also be

working in the current, and as such their continually changing profile will help the fly to appear life-like. Both of these effects are of great advantage when fish are viewing a fly against the sky.

It is therefore possible to fish with only one 'named' fly, and I know of anglers who use nothing other than a Willie Gunn tied in a selection of varying forms and sizes: in the larger sizes their flies are garish with good amounts of yellow and orange, the middle sizes have an even mix, while the smaller sizes are mostly black with very little orange or yellow.

FLY SIZE

Some anglers argue that the colour of the fly makes little difference, others that it does: I wouldn't like to say. Fly size, however, *does* make all the difference.

The Effect of Water Temperature on Fish Behaviour

It has long been established that when the water is cold – below 40°F (4.4°C) – salmon are much more likely to take a large fly (one longer than 3in/76mm) fished deep with a sinking line, than a small fly (one of 1¼in/31mm or less) fished close to the surface with a floater. Since the salmon's metabolism is directly affected by the surrounding water temperature, it stands to reason that in these circumstances a fish will be lethargic and sluggish in its movements and so will not want to move far to intercept a fly. Thus when the water temperature is below the mid 40s°F we stand a far better chance of tempting fish by presenting our flies slowly and deep.

What is Deep?

The term 'deep' in salmon fishing is frequently misunderstood. In the angling press we are told time and time again that during the early spring and late autumn months we must fish large, weighty flies *deep*, with medium to fast sinking lines. However, this approach is not always the best practice. Many anglers, and particularly those new to the sport, will interpret 'deep' as having to dredge the bottom in order to meet with success. But the depth at which salmon are found depends on the lies they take up, and I do not regard salmon to be 'deep' unless they are in more than 5ft (1.5m) of water.

Far too many anglers overemphasize the need for water depth when fishing during the spring. Even in the coldest of water, salmon will very often take up lies

In order to catch salmon in large rivers it is often essential to wade deep. One must always be cautious of disturbing fish.

in glides and streams between 2 and 5ft (0.6m and 1.5m) deep, and most anglers fishing for spring salmon will walk past these places without giving them a second thought. They do so at their own loss. For example, when fishing for a salmon lying in 5ft (1.5m) of water, our fly should be fishing at a depth of 42in (1.1m), that is, about 18in (45cm) above the fish. I have found that if a fly is presented at this distance above a fish, it will rise to take it, even in the coldest of water conditions. A salmon lying in a slow flow at this depth can be covered easily with a medium-weight fly and slow sinker. But if the lie is in only 3ft (90cm) of water, a floating or neutral density line is more suitable. The final choice, however, will be dictated by the pace of the current being fished at the time.

February on the Tay. It is not always essential to dredge the bottom. On this occasion I am fishing with an Intermediate line and 2in (50mm) Waddington.

On the subject of covering fish properly when the water is cold, Michael Evans in the 1991 August edition of *Trout & Salmon* wrote the following:

Although I accept that a very low water temperature will slow down the salmon's rate of metabolism, I don't think it has a bearing on where in a pool they might be lying. Their main concern is rest, and this is provided by the different features of the riverbed or its course. The only factor that changes, so far as the fisher is concerned, is the height of water above the fish and the speed of the current. I will therefore use whatever line, or weight of fly which is best suited to reach the fish.

Even though this literary piece was written with regard to fishing for late summer and early autumn salmon, it is equally true for spring fish.

The main reason for fishing our flies slow when the water is cold is that any indigenous aquatic river life will be slow-moving at this time, whether it be small fish, or free-swimming invertebrates. Therefore a fly fished fast at such times would be out of place compared with the sub-aquatic river life.

Correlating Fly Size to Water Temperature

As the water temperature starts to increase into the higher 40s°F, usually from the end of April onwards, salmon display a marked change in their taking behaviour: instead of preferring a large fly presented at nose level, they will rise – sometimes on occasions through many feet of water – to take the tiniest of flies fished just under the surface. Many theories have been put forward as to why this transformation in taking behaviour comes about. Only recently one writer suggested that salmon take a large fly fished deep when the water is cold because they remember feeding on fish in the deeper, colder layers of the sea; and that a small fly fished just below the surface represents the zooplankton found in the upper layers of the seas around Greenland where the salmon used to feed.

I agree with the first of these proposals; as to the zooplankton, however, I have my doubts. This is because many species of

Hook Size	Partridge Low Water Single	Partridge Low Water Double	Partridge X2B Long Shank Treble	Esmond Drury Trebles	Mustad 80525 Doubles	Mustad 80550 Trebles	Kamasan Salmon Doubles	Kamasan Salmon Trebles
2	38	33	34	36	36	37	Not made	Not made
4	32	29	28	30	34	33	34	34
6	28	26	24	26	29	30	30	29
8	23	24	20	22	26	26	25	25
10	19	20	16	18	23	22	21	23

Table 1 Hook sizes in millimetres.

zooplankton are very small, generally only a few millimetres in size, and compared to, say, a size 10 low-water double hook, are very much smaller (*see* Table 1 for hook sizes in millimetres).

Certainly salmon *do* feed on zooplankton, and it is also known that where some species are transparent, many of those which frequent the upper surface layers of open oceans where salmon are known to feed are bright blue in colour. Now, it might be conjectured that the blue throat collars found on so many of the acclaimed 'warm water flies' are there to represent the blue coloration found in these species. Perhaps they are, but to be honest I think these blue collars are nothing more than sheer coincidence – and nor do I believe that the small flies we fish near the surface during the warmer months are taken for zooplankton.

Some anglers believe that salmon rise to tiny wisps of flies with a head and tail rise when the water temperature is warm – above 48°F (8.9°C) – because it stimulates them into adopting parr-like behaviour again. I do not agree. If it does, then why don't they make a grab for everything which passes by? When the water is colder and the fish prefer a deeper fly, these same anglers also believe this behaviour is related to the feeding behaviour of the fish while at sea: these anglers therefore maintain that low water temperatures bring about a sea-feeding behaviour while higher temperatures promote a river-feeding behaviour.

My own belief as to why salmon demonstrate a dramatic change in taking behaviour for dissimilar water temperatures is this: as the water warms up the fish become more active and so become more alert, and inevitably start to focus their attention upwards, towards the surface. Although there *are* recorded instances of fish taking flies with a 4 or 5in (100 or 127mm) wing such as a Collie Dog fished fast across a pool when the water is in the high 60s°F (19–20°C), and of fish taking small (0.5in/12.5mm) Stoat's Tail-type flies when the water is in the lower 40s°F (4–6°C), these successes are not commonplace, particularly when compared to the number of fish taken by the 'accepted', established approaches for the prevailing water temperatures.

The Effect of Water Coloration

I have spoken to a number of anglers who think that the amount of diffused oxygen, suspended matter and the chemical make-up of the water at the time can also play a part in determining salmon behaviour. Personally I see no reason why this should not be so, though whether any of these could actually affect a change in taking behaviour remains to be seen. However, when rivers are running in spate, the amount of diffused oxygen and chemical composition will be different to that when the river is running at normal height. This is particularly so of rivers which run through peat and agricultural land: given rain, their chemical composition changes, the rivers which run through peat becoming decidedly more acidic, while those which run through low-lying agricultural land receive a cocktail of fertilizers and phosphates. I have found that the increased acidity which occurs in moorland rivers during a spate can make fish reluctant to come to a small fly fished just under the surface. From what I have experienced when fishing in peat-stained rivers carrying extra water, salmon at these times appear to prefer a fly fished deeper and closer. In many of the rivers which run through agricultural land, fish will not be tempted to a fly until most of the colour clears and the chemical composition of the river returns to pre-spate levels.

The reason why most fish are caught on large flies when the water is coloured is because most anglers will be using larger flies. Water coloration generally determines the size of fly the angler chooses – although there is no positive evidence to suggest that salmon prefer a large fly to a small one when the water is coloured. Salmon have excellent eyesight, and as such are capable of seeing the smallest of flies in the dirtiest of water.

Measuring Water Coloration

Recently I was reading an article on trout fishing where the author gave a chart showing the number of trout caught in relation to water coloration, and the unit for water coloration was given as 'the Hazen'. Now until I had read this article I must say I had never heard of such a unit. What I found a little strange was that the reference of 'five Hazen units' was given for gin-clear water: I would have thought that clear, uncoloured water would have had a Hazen rating of one. However, enough of my ignorance: if a graph showing Hazen units was established for each salmon river flowing under changing conditions throughout the year, I am sure it would provide us with information which would help us learn a little more about the taking behaviour of this remarkable creature. Perhaps it would even take us a little closer to understanding the taking nuances which exist between salmon in different river systems.

The Effect of Relative Air Temperature

Well kept fishing diaries of earlier generations of salmon anglers would indicate that as the water temperature increases the fly size should be reduced. Many of these records also show us that salmon prefer the water to be perceptibly colder than the air. Thus if the water and air temperatures are very similar, they show an obvious reluctance to move to a fly – or to any lure for that matter – regardless of the depth at which they are fished. However, once the air temperature rises a few degrees above that of the water, usually about 5°F (2.8°C) they will start to take an interest in what is being presented.

On occasions salmon will rise to a small fly fished only a few inches below the surface when the water temperature is hovering around the mid 40s°F. I have found that this behaviour is more likely to occur during the autumn than in the spring: during the spring it generally takes a few mild days of decent weather to bring about any positive changes in air temperatures, whereas in autumn, especially during the months of October and November and to a lesser extent September, overnight ground frosts can drastically lower water temperatures. In fact quite often at this time of the year it is necessary to employ more than one set of tactics throughout the day. Sometimes you have to start off fishing with a sinking line and large fly, but come the middle of the afternoon, if the sun makes an appearance and the water and air temperatures rise, you may have to change over to a small fly and floating line. By regularly monitoring the water and air temperatures throughout the day, and by changing over to a floater as soon as the air temperature rises above the water temperature by 5°F

(2.8°), I have frequently taken fish when other anglers who have persisted with a large, deeply fished fly have finished the day or week with a blank.

A.H.E. Wood only gave attention to water temperature when it fell to around the 40°F (4.4°C) mark; anything above this and he was more concerned about the depth, clarity and speed of the water when choosing the size of his fly. Concerning the taking of fish early in the season, he once remarked that when the water temperature was 38°F (3.3°C) he would start with a fly tied on a size 1 or 2; if he failed to move fish to either of these sizes, he would reduce the size until he caught a kelt – and having done so, he would then change up a size. This may seem like a strange approach, but if we accept that some kelts resume feeding again when descending the river, in fact it makes a great deal of sense. Then, just like today, kelts were much more plentiful than spring fish, so what better way of finding the correct size of fly for the prevailing conditions, than fishing for a fish that has started to regain its feeding habit after many months of fasting?

River banks are full of dangers. Here Mary is carefully working her way to the water's edge along an assemblage of loose boulders after some pool improvement work.

Choosing the Right Size Fly

By correlating and tabulating details of fly size to water temperatures from my own fishing diary, as well as the overall fly sizes addressed in the writings of four past and present distinguished angling authorities, I have created a graph to show the size of fly that has proved the most effective in tempting fish for a given water temperature. In order to give a true representation of these sizes I have given them in millimetres rather than hook sizes. This is for two reasons: first, the overall hook size seems to vary depending on style and manufacturer (*see* Table 1), so quoting the hook size will only lead to unnecessary confusion for a novice when he/she is trying to decide the size of fly to use. And second, the size of the hook is very often irrelevant when compared to the overall size of the fly, as the fly in question may have the dressing well past the bends of the hooks. If we look at the Ally's Shrimp, or the General Practitioner-type flies where the 'feeler' hairs extend well beyond the bend of the hook, you will see what I mean, and this is why I have given the overall fly size rather than merely quoting hook size.

Graph 1 must be taken merely as a guide, as it only shows the size of fly for normal water conditions, with the air temperature assumed at 5°F (2.8°C) higher. If the air temperature is lower than that of the water, or if a smaller differential exists between the air and water, the fly size will have to be increased in relation to the difference. Correspondingly if the difference between the two is greater than 5°F (2.8°C), the size of fly will have to be reduced. Further to this, if the river is in spate and running dirty, or alternatively if it is flowing below summer level, the temperature sizes will not apply.

We must also remember that the fly size shown is part of a much more complex equation which includes many changeable variables. For example, as the season progresses the water temperature will rise due to higher air temperatures; also the volume of water flowing will be reduced. This means of course that the pools will now be narrower, shallower and slower.

Fly Sizes for Different River Systems

Air temperature, water temperature, clarity and height are unequivocally and intrinsically linked in determining fly size. Since the graph results from the figures given by a number of anglers fishing many different rivers, the sizes given for a given set of water temperatures will inevitably vary from one river to another. Bill Currie in his book *The River Within*, wrote the following concerning the variances in fly sizes for different rivers:

The Tay fish for example, usually demand a slightly larger fly. In summer conditions on the Tay, which may look as clear as the Dee and would make me want to fish size eight or ten, I have often found that the salmon prefer a six. In May and June I have sometimes found the small one-inch Waddington, dressed with black and a mix of orange hair, to be best on the Tay. In July a size six Shrimp has scored. In August and September the story is similar, where my Dee approaches would indicate a wisp of a fly, the Tay asks for a little more substance, more dressing, a trailing tail or even a small Waddington. I have explained this to myself sometimes in terms of water clarity. The Tay is not so shiningly clear as the Dee. Then I bring myself up short with the fact that in

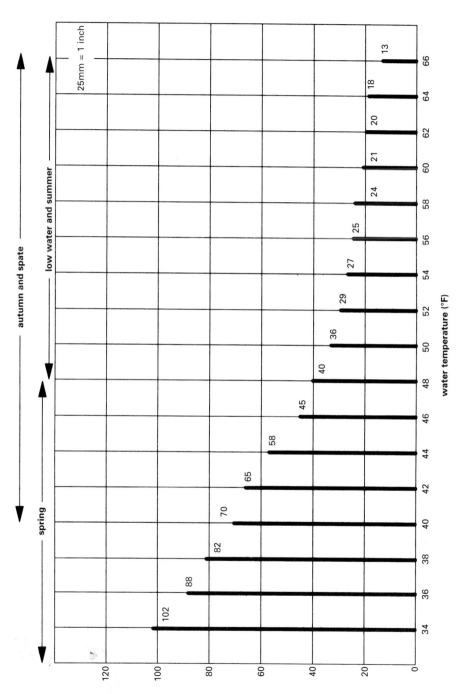

Graph 1 Fly sizes in millimetres for a given water temperature (not to scale).

a river like the summer Helmsdale, which even at its clearest is the colour of sherry, fish will sometimes only come to a ten or a twelve... If the variations, river to river, were only in the order of a couple of hook sizes, that would perhaps be containable. From time to time however, I fish waters where the taking size may be so grossly different that I begin to look for special reasons.

Where there is no doubt that the size of flies can vary enormously from one river system to another, in some rivers it can also vary within beats. Generally on most rivers the further upstream you go, the smaller the fly you should use, although the reverse seems to be the case on the Beauly: this is because the water temperature on the upper beats is colder than on the lower river below Kilmorack Dam, and as a result, anglers fishing above the Aigas Dam need flies that are one or two sizes larger (the distance between both dams being no more than three miles). On the whole, however, experience over the years has shown me that the further upstream on a river one fishes, the smaller the fly one needs to use in order to interest fish. Having said this, fresh salmon in tidal water, or in the first freshwater holding pool, have frequently demonstrated that they prefer a tiny wisp of a fly to a large one.

The Effect of Wind on Fish Behaviour

I know of two notable Highland rivers of equal stature which are separated by only a few miles, where the size of fly preferred by anglers fishing one river is almost twice the length favoured by those fishing on the other. One angler I know who fishes both the rivers in question regularly, recently suggested to me that perhaps the reason for this anomaly is the differing wind factors affecting each river system, one having a windier valley than the other. Since a sudden rise of wind ruffling the surface of a loch can suddenly and inexplicably bring fish on the take, I see no reason why it cannot have a similar effect on rivers. A cold wind dying away can, and frequently does, bring a pool alive with fish, which only moments before showed no signs of life at all: on more than one occasion I have been fishing when there has been a bitterly cold easterly or northerly wind blowing and seen not a fin during my efforts; yet if that wind drops, the whole atmosphere changes instantly, and fish will start to show – if I am still fishing at this time and have not sought sanctuary in the hut, I have frequently found myself becoming attached to a fish. This sort of incident has happened to me too often to be mere coincidence.

If a sudden blow of wind gets up and then dies away equally as quickly, this often has a similar effect to a cold wind dying away – that is, both occurrences seem to bring fish on the take. And if the wind can thus bring fish on the take, then it is reasonable to suppose it could also play a part in determining the size of fly. However, experimentation would have to be conducted, along with accurately kept records of events over a long period of time, before we could come to any conclusions on the issue. It would be possible to monitor the effects that an increase in wind velocity, or the sudden arrival of a 'wee blow' has on fly size, as these winds usually last a usable amount of time. However, the sudden dying away of a cold wind generally lasts a very short time, sometimes only a few seconds, and because of this, any experimentation with fly sizes is just not possible.

It is good practice to slide fish up the bank before attempting to lift, especially a heavy one.

Putting the Theory into Practice

Even though Graph 1 is somewhat limited, it can still be put to good use. Suppose the river is in spate, with an extra 18in (46cm) on the gauge and running murky: first of all take the water temperature in the usual way so as to determine the size of fly required for normal conditions (the river running with normal height and clarity). Having done this, we now select a fly for a much lower water temperature. For example, during the warmer months of the season – from about mid-May through to the end of October – I have found that with a substantial increase in water height, more than

12in (30cm), a fly for a water temperature 6°F (3.4°C) lower is about right, i.e. about 2°F (1.1°C) for every 1in (2.5cm) rise. And if the water is also running turbid, a further increase in fly size will be needed: for instance when it is running 'thick', choose a fly for a water temperature an additional 6°F (3.4°C) lower; when 'cloudy' another 4°F (2.2°); and 2°F (1.1°C) when it is running the colour of strong tea.

This means that if the water temperature was 56°F (13°C) and the table suggested a 1in (25mm) fly for normal conditions, if there was a 12in (30cm) dirty spate our fly would have to be increased to 2¼in

(58mm). By adopting this approach you will discover that the size of fly will either increase or decrease by a little over a factor of two, i.e. double or half in size. Some writers will tell you to go up one hook size – about the equivalent of only 2°F (1.1°C) on the graph – when the water is high and coloured, and to come down by the same amount when the water is low and clear. I must stress that I have found that this is not very productive: if the water is below normal height, warm and running clear, I have found that halving the size of my fly is much more likely to produce fish. However, as is always the case when salmon fishing, one must always be vigilant and take note of any changes in water height and temperatures that might occur throughout the day. This is especially so with spate rivers, as some have a tendency to rise and fall very fast, or when fishing rivers which suffer from snowmelt during the spring.

In short, when the water level starts falling, or if the water temperature increases, reduce your size of fly. Conversely if the water height increases, or the water temperature takes a downward turn increase your fly size accordingly. When the water temperature is very cold (34°F; 1.1°C) and the river is flowing with some extra height, it is virtually impossible to fish effectively with a fly rod since we would need a fly well in excess of 6in (150mm). At this time, instead of increasing the size of our fly, it might well pay to put on one of the same size but with a superior visibility factor. This is assuming we are fishing with a fly 4in (102mm) long, and since I don't like fishing with flies any larger than this, I will, if a larger lure is called for, opt for the spinning rod.

Alternatively when the river is very low and warm, there is no doubt that 'small' is best. At this time it is best to use a single-handed rod with small flies. I have occasionally taken salmon on size 14 bronze wee double trout hooks, i.e. about ½in (12mm), when fishing for trout, but when fishing for salmon in earnest with either the single- or double-handed rod, I seldom go below a size 12 Esmond Drury treble, i.e. ¾in (15mm). The smallest fly on which I myself have seen a salmon taken was a size 16 trout double. As well as this it was very lightly dressed, a wisp of a thing, having only four or five black squirrel hairs tied in above and below the shank to form a wing and false beard. The fish came from a very low River Dulnain (a tributary of the Spey) by Graham Dunsmure, who was fishing the last light of an early July evening for sea-trout. At such times when the water is warm and running low and clear; we must fish tiny flies in order to give ourselves the best chance of a salmon.

FLY SPEED

Mention the greased line method of fishing for salmon, and the name A.H.E. Wood instantly comes to mind. Other eminent greased line anglers of the time included such gentlemen as W.J. Barry, E.M. Crossfield, Arthur Hutton and Anthony Crossley, all of whom corresponded regularly with Wood on many aspects of catching salmon on fly. Some will say that having unlimited access to possibly the most prolific beat in the country at the time had a lot to do with Arthur Wood's outstanding success. Perhaps it did; however, Wood was without doubt an innovator and a thinker, and it was by approaching the sport with these qualities that helped establish him as one of the 'great' salmon fishers. He believed that of all things in salmon fishing, the water height was of the utmost importance if any chance of sport was to be had. This was evident by the fact that he had a water height gauge installed into the study at Cairnton Lodge so that the exact height of the river could be checked without leaving the house.

The Greased Line Technique of Arthur Wood

Much has been written about Wood's greased line technique by other authors, though their interpretation of it is often wrong: Wood knew only too well that a fish would not take something that was moving in a unnatural manner, and his intention was not to have his flies come across the fish side on, and in a lifeless drifting fashion – it was all about control-ling the drag, and as we all know, this is achieved more easily the closer a line is fished to the surface. This is where the plastic-coated, modern-day, full floating line gives us a level of control that Wood could only have dreamt about. I believe the greased lines with which Wood, Lam-ing, and Grant fished were probably the equivalent to the 3M Scientific Wet Cel Intermediate lines available today.

The technique when greasing the old braided silk lines was to grease almost their entire length apart from the last yard or two. This being the case, the fly was not as close to the surface as some might think. I am sure that fishing the fly close to the surface was only secondary as far as Wood was concerned, the prime objective being the control factor: it was the fly's speed which was of paramount impor-tance. The braided silk lines used by Wood

did not stay floating for very long, and so he always fished with several rods set up and ready for use. The greased lines he used would float relatively well in slow unbroken water, but in a stream with any pace at all they soon sank. This is why he had several rods ready to use, because at that time Cairnton had a great deal of streamy water.

Shortly after Woods purchased Cairn-ton Lodge he had all the old jetties rebuilt as well as some new ones. This was for two reasons: first, he did not like to wade; and second, he thought that by being above the water he would see his fly more easily and as a result control it better: by fishing from these vantage points he could see every movement of fish and fly in the crystal-clear waters of the Dee. It is because of the observations he made from these jetties that many angling writers have been led to interpret his style wrong-ly: many believed that the majority of fish which came to Wood's flies broke the sur-face with a classic head and tail rise, because he wrote about 'seeing salmon rise and take his flies when fishing the greased line'. This is certainly so, and he *did* see them rise to his flies; but many of them did not break the surface, they were merely seen to rise 'through' the water from the vantage provided by the jetties.

Further, when writing to other eminent anglers of the time, Arthur Wood com-mented that he loved to 'see fish breaking the surface as they rose to his flies': and it is due to these writings that some anglers think his flies were fished just sub-surface. However, as I mentioned previously, the line used at the time did not facilitate the same shallow fishing of flies that we can achieve today. The Dee is not a deep river, and Dee fish are free rising (compared to

Fishing a fly in the quieter slower water along the edge when a river is in spate often brings reward.

some rivers). I believe that Wood's flies were actually deeper in the water than the 3 to 6in (76 to 150mm) suggested by some experts. With modern-day, high-floating plastic lines it is relatively easy to fish flies at this depth, but I feel it would have been

very difficult with the old greased lines of yesteryear. In addition, the flies were very lightly dressed on the front third of the hook and because of this, the tendency would be for them to fish deeper in the water than today's modern hairwing equivalents; also, they would receive very little upward lift from the current.

Wood discovered from his fishing that the speed of the fly in relation to its size was of paramount importance. For instance, he found that the only effective way to fish a small fly was to present it at a speed which would be natural to a creature of similar size, and that the best way of achieving this was to use a line that was on or close to the surface. As mentioned earlier, he was not the first to fish the greased line; but by taking a method and adapting it, he found a way of achieving what he wanted to do.

Whether one admires Wood and his practices or not, one thing is certain: his place in angling history is secure, because if nothing else he was a thinking angler, and there are far too few of these nowadays.

Factors Affecting Fly Speed

Fly speed is related to four things: water temperature, fly size, the pace of the current being fished, and the method of presentation. Water temperature not only affects the salmon, it also has an effect on the mobility and swimming speed of the other sub-aquatic life in the river as well. Consequently the pace of the current in which the entity is swimming will also determine its maximum speed. It therefore stands to reason that it is easier for a 2in (50mm) minnow to maintain its position in a fast current than one of half that size. So when fishing a fly – whether it is in the spring or summer – it is essential to have an idea of what the maximum swimming speed for a creature of the same size as the fly we are fishing is likely to be for the prevailing water conditions.

Although the size of the fly we use will dictate the maximum swimming speed it can be fished, its size will not dictate the depth at which it can be fished: a large fly does not necessarily have to be fished deep, or a small fly fished just sub-surface to attract salmon. The only reason during the spring for fishing with a large fly deep and presenting it at a slow speed right in front of the salmon's nose, is that when the water is cold, salmon seldom want to move far to take a lure. Conversely when the water warms up, a Collie Dog with a 4in (100mm) wing stripped back fast just under the surface will often tempt a fish that has refused a small fly presented in the 'conventional' fashion for the prevailing conditions.

A long-winged Collie Dog swimming fast through a pool just under the surface scores with spring salmon from a number of Highland rivers, the fish very often coming to it with a great vortexing swirl. Neil Graesser invented the fly, and stated that the Collie Dog would not work unless the water temperature was above 42°F (5.6°C). One reason put forward for this behaviour is that salmon are more prepared to surmount temperature barriers at this temperature.

However, experience over the years has shown me that there are no exactitudes when it comes to the behaviour of salmon, and as such I view such definitive statements with more than a little bit of scepticism. In addition, when the water is warm and low, a small fly inched slowly back along the bottom will also take fish. As far as I am concerned, the reason that all these approaches attract fish is that the fly happens to be moving in a fashion and at a speed that the salmon accept as being natural.

Choosing the Right Size Fly
for the Flow

In my opinion most anglers change their flies too often, generally because they lose faith in it. Moreover, when they change flies it is normally for one of a different colour, and not size, and I believe that this is a great mistake. Most pools do not have a uniform flow through them, and in order to fish them properly an angler may have to change the size of his fly a number of times. For most situations, and whether we are fishing a large or a small fly, we strive to present them as slowly as possible. We must therefore present the fish with the size of fly that looks as if it is capable of holding station within the flow in which it is being fished.

Most creatures will only venture into flows in which they are capable of controlling their progress; those entering a flow which is overpowerful for them will get washed away downstream where they may be killed, or injured by being slammed against stones or rocks. This is why it is important to fish the 'appropriate' size of fly for the flow being fished and it often means changing fly sizes two, three or even four times when fishing down a pool, the number of times depending on the variances of the flows within the pool in question. In the fast, streamy water at the head of a pool I would opt for a slightly larger fly than the water temperature suggests, then as I near the belly of the pool I will change to a smaller one.

If you do not want to change flies as you progress down the pool, another method I sometimes employ is to fish with the same size of fly from head to tail, but at different speeds. By following this practice, though, I have had to educate myself to become aware of the subtle nuances of current flow which will affect my fly's passage across the pool. Any changes of water pace will of course affect the maximum potential swimming speed of the fly: thus in the faster headstream, the fly you are fishing may only appear 'right' to the salmon if it looks as if it can just hold position in the flow. Thus as you start to fish the belly of the pool, do not present the fly at the same shallow angle as you employed in the head of the stream, because if you do, its water speed may now not be enough to keep it swimming attractively – it may start to sink and lose its semblance of life.

Finally, in order to keep the fly attractive in the slower sections of the pool, its water speed must be increased; by doing this it will look much more natural to any fish present. This is because as the fly comes into the slower water, any salmon which has been taking an interest in it and has followed it round out of the current will expect its speed to increase. And if a fish was following our fly at this point, any reduction in its water speed will almost certainly cause it to lose interest. Thus very often an increase in fly speed, whether it is actual or relative to a following fish, will provoke it into taking. On nearing the tail of the pool the fly's speed must once again be slowed down to create the desired illusion, i.e. that of a smal creature maintaining its water speed.

Changing Line Density

When fishing a pool, very few anglers change either their flies or their presentation speed to suit the flow. If we are to fish a pool 'properly', however, not only must the size of the fly be changed, but on occasions we may have to change the fly line as well. One of the easiest ways of presenting our fly at a consistent depth is not only to put on flies of different sizes as we fish down the pool, but of different weight as well. Some pools will require more than one line density in order for us to fish them properly. Therefore if you have more than one rod and can be bothered carrying them, I suggest you set up two rods with differing line ratings. There are many pools where more than two lines will be needed, and by changing rods and flies when fishing these pools you will stand a better chance of taking a fish than someone who merely fishes from head to tail with the same line and fly. I know, two rods are nuisance to carry about all day – however, if you are only allocated a short stretch where the pools are relatively close, two rods can be put to great advantage.

Now suppose, for example, we want to fish a fly at a depth of between 9 and 12in (23 and 30cm): the line needed initially will depend on the pool in question and the pace of the current. Suppose we are fishing a long wide pool on the River Spey: the head of the pool is fast, with the fish-holding water 25 yards (23m) or more in the slacker water on the far edge of the stream. Very often a fly fished with a floating line will skate in this situation so in order to have our flies fishing at the required depth here, a sinking line of medium density may be required, and if the flow is extremely hard, a full sinking line may be necessary. As we fish our way down the pool the speed of the current will start to diminish, and as our flies begin to fish this section, a neutral density, or intermediate-type line will be better suited. As we near the slowest section of the pool we may very well have to change over to a full floating line. And near the tail where the

speed of the current will be increasing, it may be necessary to change back to a line of neutral density.

The type of lines needed for each situation cannot be learned from a book: experience alone will determine the correct line. One final point is that the sinking rate (SR) of sinking lines differs from one manufacturer to another – thus a sinker of one make will be quite different from another. For example, Airflo Glass Intermediate lines are currently the slowest sink lines on the market (as far as I am aware) sinking at 0.75–1in (19–25mm)/sec, while the Wet Cel Intermediate is rated between 1.25–1.75in (31–44mm)/sec. The Wet Cel ll, categorized as a fast sinker, has a sinking rate of between 1.75–3.00in (44–75mm)/sec (the greatest sink distance per second being recorded in a virtual no flow situation). Having looked at the sinking rates of two Wet Cel lines, we see a Wet Cel Intermediate in a slow flow will sink the same distance per second as a Wet Cel ll will in a strong flow.

Not only does the sinking rate and current determine the depth a line will sink, the length of line being used will also determine the depth our flies will fish. Thus, on a large, wide river we may need to use an intermediate, while on a smaller river a fast sinker will be needed to make our flies swim at the same depth. I believe the depth at which a fly is fished is as important as the size of fly being fished. Unfortunately this aspect is often forgotten by other writers.

Fly Speed in Relation to Water Speed

At this point I was going to give a range of fly speeds categorized from 1 to 5 (1 being the slowest) indicating how each size of fly should be fished for best effect. However, I have come to the conclusion that this would be very difficult, if not downright impossible. I have therefore decided to use the 1 to 5 range not for identifying the speed at which each size of fly should be fished, but to try and simplify the aspect of relevant fly speed by relating it to actual water speed. For explanation purposes, assume we have allowed our fly to come to the dangle, when it will be swimming at the same speed as that of the current; in the range we will identify it as having a rating of 3. Now assume that we have cast our line at 45 degrees across the pool and put in an upstream mend: the fly will start to swim across the stream at a slower speed than the current in which it is swimming; it now has a speed rating of 2. If we stand our ground and make the next cast from the same place, but execute two upstream mends instead of one, our fly will have an even slower speed than it acquired on its first passage.

Having said this, the amount of line mended and the time at which each are executed must be precise: if we do not mend the correct quantity of line, or if the mends are executed at the wrong time, we will not produce the desired speed. If we execute the upstream mends properly our fly should now have a speed rating of 1, that is, approximately half what it was before. Some of you will be saying that if the fly swims too slowly it will sink: this is correct. When fishing with the floating line, too large a mend, or too many mends, will cause the fly to sink and fish deeper. However, this does not create too much of a problem, especially with a floater, as the buoyancy of the line helps to keep the fly relatively high in the water. Nonetheless, too large a mend and the fly may lose some

of its attractiveness. Moreover too large an upstream mend, or too many mends when fishing a sinking line, is much more serious because the fly will indeed sink and as a result will start snaring the bottom, or worse still a salmon. This is why when fishing a sinking line it is essential to know the amount of mending required to keep the fly swimming properly.

Next I shall look at how we can create an increase in our fly's speed in relation to relevant water speed. Again assume the fly has come to the dangle: if we now pull in a few yards of line, the fly will move upstream. The fly now has a positive speed in relation to the current and would register as 4 or 5 on the speed range scale depending on how fast it is pulled upstream. The same effect can be achieved by casting 45 degrees across the pool and putting in a downstream mend. By doing this the current will take hold of the line and pull the fly across the pool at a faster pace than the speed of the flow in which it is being fished. The greater the downstream mend, the faster the fly will fish. However, if too much of a downstream mend is executed when using a floating line, it could result in the fly fishing overfast for its size. When performed with a sinking line the fly's water speed will also increase. However, provided it is still swimming at a speed obtainable for a creature of similar size within such a flow, all will be well. Very often if a downstream mend is executed at the right place in the flow the increase in fly speed brought about by it often encourages a hesitant fish which has been following to move forward and take with conviction.

To recap: upstream mending will decrease a fly's swimming speed, while downstream mending will increase it.

3 A CHANGE OF FLY

SOME POINTERS TO FLY SELECTION

I do believe that provided one has selected the size of fly established by previous generations to be the most likely to produce sport for the prevailing conditions, there is very little to be gained from constantly changing the flies you are using. All this does is waste valuable fishing time. I let a friend fish my rod one evening on a productive beat: up till then he had never caught a salmon on the fly, and since the beat was stuffed with fish I thought it ideal. I regret to say he did not catch anything. He rose fish, but touched none. Having fished the beat in question now for a number of years I have come to know that when the fish in it show interest in a fly, what is called for is a change of presentation, and not of the fly. During the course of the evening he was constantly changing flies, in fact I lost count of the changes – as the old adage says, only a fly which is being fished can catch fish. Even so it is very difficult to justify to novice anglers not to change, especially when their enthusiasm for their choices starts to wane. Nevertheless, until you get positive evidence that the fly being used is fishing badly, or is the wrong size – too large or too small – it is best to keep to the original.

It is advisable before starting to fish any pool to spend some time reconnoitring the water you are about to fish, especially if you have never fished the stretch before. While doing so, decisions can be made regarding tackle and tactics: line densities and rods can generally be decided quickly, but when establishing your choice of fly take your time. Try tying one or two on to a length of nylon and dangling them in the flow to see how they react. Although a fly may look 'right' when placed in the hand or sitting in a fly box, it often has a tendency to look very different once submerged and tethered to a leader. It may be that there is insufficient flow to make it appealing to fish, in which case a smaller or a more mobile alternative will have to be selected. Note that a smaller fly does not necessarily mean it will have greater mobility than a large one, and how mobile a fly is does not just depend on the size and style of hook to which it is tied (I will cover this point later in the chapter): the material from which the wing is constructed plays a major role, too. The first indication one usually gets that a fly is too large is when someone else takes a fish or two on a smaller one; other indications are fish which follow, slash, splash, tweak or turn away from the fly we are offering them. Sometimes if these fish are presented with a smaller one they may on occasions come again – although there are no guarantees when it comes to salmon fishing: very often a fish which has shown interest in our initial offering will offer no further response regardless of what we next show it. The decision whether or not to change to a smaller fly is a personal one; sometimes it works, sometimes it doesn't. If fishing a river when there are plenty of fresh fish showing, I feel that a change of fly as policy after just one 'missed bite' is not realistic. On the other hand, if I start experiencing a succession of 'half-hearted' fish I will have no hesitation in changing the size of my fly.

Shrimp-type Flies

Some anglers fish with prawn- or shrimp-type pattern flies, believing that in order to produce a response from a fish its feeding memory must be activated. These flies when fished slowly across a pool with the standard down-and-across approach take countless fish throughout a season. Not all anglers have found similar success, however: I recall a chat with an eminent angling writer I met while having a few days' fishing on the Bladnoch. After fishing together for a while he expressed interest in my preference for using shrimp-type flies having not had particular success with them himself: for instance, whenever he fished with a two-fly set-up which included a shrimp pattern, if he hooked a fish it would always be on the other fly and not the shrimp pattern, regardless of whether it was fished on the point or dropper position.

A number of anglers when fishing these patterns prefer to fish them by raising and lowering their rod points, while others will retrieve them as they swing across the pool with an erratic, jerky sink-and-draw action; this last practice probably best represents the swimming action of the natural shrimp or prawn.

Elver Flies

Richard Waddington in his book *Salmon Fishing, A New Philosophy*, first published in 1947, rejected all the common beliefs for a salmon taking a fly such as aggression or curiosity, and proposed that salmon took an angler's fly simply out of habit. He subsequently went on to suggest that the elver of the European eel could be a staple food item of the salmon at sea.

Arthur Ransome must also have thought the same, because he developed the Elver fly to represent these small creatures. They are constructed with the wings tied in along the top of the hook like a reservoir streamer fly. By sitting the feathers at right-angles to the flow, the current will act on them in such a way as to represent the side-to-side motion of a small fish or elver swimming through the water. Although this fly was initially intended to be fished in the conventional down-and-across fashion in a fast stream, it has for some odd reason been adopted as a dapping fly!

MAKING A FLY LOOK ALIVE

The reason why both shrimp and elver flies, or any other flies for that matter, bring success is because they look alive. If something acts as if it's alive, then it probably is as far as the fish is concerned. By using materials in the tying of a fly which in the water will most closely simulate the way a live creature moves, you will greatly increase its attractiveness. One technique is to use wing and throat materials that are limited to specific flows. Thus in a slow flow, soft, easily influenced hair in conjunction with a soft false hackle will produce the best effect. However, if fished in a fast current these flies will produce an unattractive, 'dead' profile because the current will push the hair and hackles flat against the hook shank; thus when fishing fast streamy water a fly with a stiffish hair and a full throat hackle is best. These fibres work very well in a good strong current, but in a slow flow they will appear stiff and inanimate.

Choosing Monofilament to Complement the Fly

The type of monofilament you select contributes a great deal to the spirit of the fly in the water. Thus if a fly is tied onto nylon whose diameter is too thick for its size, it will appear dead in the water. For a fly to fish correctly it must be used with a gauge of nylon that will allow the gradations present within the current to work upon it; thus a small fly tied to a 'heavy' gauge monofilament will not rise and dance within the flow. Note that it is not the overall size of the fly which determines the nylon, it is the weight of the 'iron' to which the dressing of the fly is tied. (The same also applies to tubes and Waddington shanks.)

It may be thought that a double hook will need a thinner diameter nylon than a treble of the same size for the fly to fish properly; however, having carried out experiments with Partridge Low Water doubles code Q1 and Partridge X2B trebles, I did not find this to be the case. Perhaps the reason for this is that the doubles are longer, size for

size, than the trebles and as a result create more lift. From my experiments I have compiled a table showing which gauge of monofilament performed best with each size of hook (*see* Table 2).

Since I have no proof that salmon are less 'gut'-shy than trout, I like to give them the benefit of the doubt and fish with nylon which I think will be the least noticeable to them. When it comes to makes I prefer Maxima – although I must admit that there have been occasions when fishing low water during bright overhead conditions when the Maxima Chameleon (brown-coloured) monofilament has stood out like a sore thumb. When fishing large flies deep when the water is cold, or on the high side and coloured, I use the Chameleon nylon; however, when fishing small flies near the surface, or in low water with bright, cloudless overhead conditions, I opt for Maxima Ultra Green. Another make I like to use is Formula 80: this nylon is clear, but it has a thicker diameter for the equivalent breaking strain compared to the Maxima.

Hook size to monofilament gauge/strain (maxima)	
Hook size	Monofilament
2	0.42mm/20lb
4	0.40mm/18lb
6	0.37mm/15lb
8	0.32mm/12lb
10	0.30mm/10lb
12	0.25mm/8lb
14	0.22mm/6lb
(Hooks: Partridge Long Shank Trebles code X2B)	

Table 2.

Ways to Increase Mobility

One modern trend to increase a fly's mobility factor is to incorporate a long wing or tail, the Ally's Shrimp and Collie Dog taking this fashion to the extreme. It has also become popular on standard hairwing patterns to extend the wing beyond the bends of the hooks as well. These flies have an attractiveness in water which the short hairwinged flies lack, although the additional hair creates more lift so they swim higher in the water. I have noticed that anglers who fish for salmon in lochs do not seem to worry about pattern nearly as much as their river-fishing counterparts. Why this is so I am not sure, but they are usually happy to fish standard loch or sea-trout type flies such as a Goat's Toe or a Black Pennell. Perhaps it is because for most of the time they are fishing with the single-handed rods and tackle they would use for trout, and by fishing in such a manner they can more easily

When anglers change their flies, many seem to forget that their leader may have to be replaced as well, especially if a different-sized fly is used.

impart the necessary life to attract attention. Generally their flies are fished as slowly as possible, and presented either just under the surface or bobbed along the top of the waves like a scurrying insect. These techniques on a loch will very often produce more interest than a fly stripped back fast beneath the surface. As far as most loch anglers are concerned fly patterns are usually of secondary importance, and they place more significance on imparting the essential life-like actions into their flies with rod and line. Perhaps river anglers should take a leaf out of the loch anglers' book.

A QUESTION OF CAMOUFLAGE

Adding further confusion to the issue of fly selection, some anglers believe that in order to be successful when fishing a river they need to fish the pattern or style of fly specific for the river in question. This is based on the theory that these flies evolved with specific characteristics to tone in with the particular river bed colour, water tint and so on of the rivers they inhabit; their own unique colorations help protect them from being seen and preyed upon. The reasoning behind using a fly which is in harmony with the surrounding river bed or water colour is so that it will appear natural to the fish, that is, the flies used would not be conspicuous by their presence. Now this is a sound argument provided we are fishing our fly on an eyeball-to-eyeball basis with the fish, or when fishing a fly deep in the water during the spring, or when trying to intercept running fish when the river is in spate; however, many of the camouflage aficionados incorporate dark, solid-colour body materials in their mid-

water and upper-water flies, and as the fish will be viewing them from beneath, they will appear dark regardless of the colour. Personally I like most of my own mid- and deep-water flies to have a gold tinsel rib, rather than silver. I think a gold rib is better suited to flies fished 'down' in the water, because I believe it to be more harmonious with the colours expected at that depth, due to the diffused light.

Most free-swimming creatures, particularly fish which frequently swim in the middle and upper layers, have a dark colour on their upper body and a lighter colour on their lower flanks, silver or white. The reason for having such a difference is to counteract the reflections from the upper surface due to the greater light shining from above, (otherwise known as obliterative graduation); silvery flanks behave like a mirror and reflect the bottom, and as a result fish with such coloration have a tendency to 'disappear' when viewed from the side. Mirror camouflage is particularly effective from most angles, although it fails somewhat when viewed directly from below: in this instance it matters little whether it has a 'solid' or reflective body. The advocates of 'camouflage' seem to forget these aspects when preaching their beliefs. Perhaps instead of using solid, dark colours in the flies they use for their mid-water fishing they should be using a silver-based tinsel to help make their flies appear more convincing to the salmon. When fishing a small subsurface fly I like to use one which has a silver rib; this I feel helps to represent the shimmering scales reflecting light off the flanks of a small fish, or the oxygen bubbles which frequently get trapped along the body of shrimps and aquatic invertebrates.

FAVOURED FLY PATTERNS

Very often a fly will be developed for one particular river system. Generally this is not by intention, but is the result of sheer chance: what usually happens is that someone happens to tie something differing from the conventional colour or style previously used on the river, gives it a swim and proceeds to catch fish. Very soon everybody is fishing with the new fly and catching fish as well. The initial reason for them being so successful is that the fish have usually been seeing the same old patterns day in, day out and then suddenly this new something swims past and attracts their attention. These flies are then fished to the exclusion of almost everything else for a season or two; inevitably they catch fish, and as a result they become synonymous with the river in question. Spey-type flies are a typical example: these are usually fairly slim, sparsely tied, dull creations consisting of Black Heron hackles palmered along the body with a small section of Bronze Mallard feather for a wing. Although there are now a great number of different Spey patterns, they are probably all bastardized copies of the original which happened to get all the attention to start with.

Sometimes a fly pattern appears in a monthly periodical and within a short period of time achieves recognition which exceeds all expectation. This is what happened with the Ally's Shrimp; there is probably not a salmon river in the UK where this fly has not accounted for fish. I think the main reason for its outstanding success is due to the publicity it received and the number of anglers fishing it. The more anglers who fish a fly the more fish it will take: as the old adage goes, 'Success breeds

success'. In fact I don't think any fly has a 'magic' colour pattern or style – its success is simply related to its frequency of use, and by looking at the different beliefs held by certain famous anglers we will see that this is so. Thus A.H.E. Wood preferred a fly style with a solid wing and slim profile dressed on a single hook. When fishing during the summer he liked his flies to be as thin as possible – at times they were so worn and tattered that all that remained on the hook was a body along with two or three hairs as wings. He referred to these 'well worn' flies as Nymphs.

How things have changed, because the style of fly that Wood developed has now passed out of favour with many of today's anglers, the majority preferring a more mobile hairwinged pattern instead. In fact he did not think pattern made much difference, but considered size of much greater importance. J.A. Hutton asked him why he only used two flies, a Blue Charm and a Silver Blue. Wood replied that he didn't care which he used. J.A. Hutton then asked him why then he did not use a March Brown, a fly not commonly used at the time for salmon fishing. To this Wood replied that he would use nothing else for the rest of the season, which he did – and took the same number of fish as he would normally have expected to catch during a season. Near the end of his life he only ever fished with a Blue Charm or March Brown.

Esmond Drury, famous for his long shank, fly tying treble and the General Practitioner prawn fly (which he invented in 1953), preferred a short, simple tying for most of his floating line work. And Arthur Oglesby, probably the best known contemporary angling instructor and writer in the UK, believes that fly patterns do not matter too much. He believes that if

Tailing a summer fish from the River Doon.

the fly being used is of the right size for the conditions and fished with the proper amount of animation it will attract fish. Having read his book *Fly Fishing for Salmon and Sea Trout* as well as many of the articles he has written over the years, I have a suspicion that the Munro Killer is a private popular choice, especially when he is fishing the Spey. In an article which appeared in the 1991 August edition of *Trout & Salmon*, Arthur Oglesby wrote the following concerning fly pattern, colour and size:

Although I am not convinced that the pattern of fly matters all that much, if you encounter low, clear water ... it makes sense to select flies which are not too garish. Almost everything in nature which is preyed upon by other creatures has the ability to melt in with its background and use its natural camouflage to best effect. In selecting my flies, therefore, I like to examine the overall colour of the riverbed, the clarity of the water and its temperature ... The Spey and Tweed, for instance, tend to be an overall dark-brown colour ... My Spey patterns therefore tend to be black or brown, with such flies as the Munro Killer, Thunder and Lightning and Stoat's Tail the first choice ... Also I have long held the view that in any salmon river, the smaller the flies we choose the more subdued they should be in colour.

Crawford Little, on the other hand, believes that on occasions the pattern can make all the difference, especially when fishing in conditions which are far from ideal, or on hard-fished association waters. In an article entitled 'A Selection for Salmon' he wrote:

> Modern salmon-fishing lore, as preached over the past few decades, states that the pattern of fly which we fish is relatively unimportant. Well, I am afraid I disagree. I cannot for the life of me accept that a change from a size 6 hook to a size 8 is all important, but that the dressing on the hook can be virtually ignored. The more areas I visit, the more rivers I fish and the more practical fishermen and gillies with whom I come into contact and discuss such things, the more I am convinced that pattern is as important ... I will not say more ... as the choice of size.

Some of the flies he likes to use are Arndilly Fancy, Bourrach and the Munro Killer. He also likes to use the Jungle Buck – highly visible fly invented by himself – during the summer and autumn when the water is high or coloured. 'His' fly comes in two versions, standard and long wing, and he particularly likes to fish it with a sinking line and long rod so he can hover it in the slower flowing stretches where running fish are known to stop for a breather. On seeing my 'high water box',

he referred to my tubes and Waddingtons as the 'Rocky Horror Show' – though I think he was referring to their colour scheme, and not their tying!

Reg Righyni considered that too many modern salmon flies presented too bold an image, and that a more nebulous fly would be far superior to anything attainable with conventional hairwing patterns. He also believed that some colours could be seen better in some colours of water and with different light intensities than others. He liked flies with a touch of colour in them such as the tried and tested Thunder and Lightning, or the Logie. In an article which appeared in the summer 1985 edition of *Gamefisher & Fly-tying Quarterly* he remarked that in his opinion it was 'dangerous' to use black flies at the exclusion of everything else; he preferred a fly which had contrasting coloured wings and bodies, to one of uniform colour. His first choice of fly for greased line fishing was always one which would present the fish with a subtle image, one that was not too vivid. To this end he used single hooks, and tied the wing and beard using hackle fibres rather than hair.

Francis Grant, on the other hand, author of *Salmon Fly Fishing – The Dynamics Approach*, favours two patterns, a Hairy Mary variant and a Drowned Mouse in a wide assortment of sizes . He emphasizes that the Hairy Mary should be lightly dressed, while the Drowned Mouse, a Willie Gunn variant, should have a long red tail incorporated into it, this helping to keep it swimming true and level in the horizontal plane. He uses the Hairy Mary primarily for his floating line work, while the Drowned Mouse is reserved for the sinking line. It is interesting to note that the Drowned

Mouse and Crawford Little's Jungle Buck both contain orange and yellow to differing degrees: even though both anglers know that salmon have excellent eyesight and can see the smallest fly in the dirtiest of water, both like to use flies which have a relatively high visibility factor when the water is cold or turbid.

Francis Grant's Hairy Mary variants are tied on tubes and small trebles with the hairs stopping just past the ends of the hooks, while the Drowned Mouse is tied exclusively on brass tubes, with the hair extending well beyond the end of them. Although anglers will fervently defend their own reasoning for choosing a particular fly, I doubt if it makes much difference to the salmon. As far as the novice is concerned, he/she will not go far wrong by following Francis Grant's advice:

> Using only one pattern saves time that otherwise would be wasted changing flies, and frees one from the weight of the extra boxes that would have to be carried to provide a full range of different sizes in different patterns. It also prevents me worrying about whether I am using the right pattern or not, something that might otherwise unsettle concentration and confidence.

(From *Salmon Fly Fishing – The Dynamics Approach* by Francis Grant, published 1993, by courtesy of Swan Hill Press).

THE SUCCESSFUL TECHNIQUE

Having looked at the beliefs of Arthur Oglesby, Crawford Little, Reg Righyni, Francis Grant *and* myself, you are probably asking who is correct: the answer to this is quite simply that we *all* are and that the reason for our successes with differing choices of fly fished during comparable conditions is very simple – it is that we are fishing flies we have the greatest faith in. Provided the angler employs the following '*Five C Rule*', he or she will catch fish: (1) **Cast competently**; (2) **Concentrate** on what he/she is doing; (3) **Control** the passage of his/her flies through the pool; (4) Have **confidence** in his/her choice of fly; and (5) **continue** fishing, and persevere even when others have called it a day. If I was asked to pick out the one which I think most likely to bring fish to the bank I would have to say rule (5), the 'sticking at it' approach. From my experience over the years this has probably accounted for the largest percentage of all fish hooked. Perhaps 'sticking at it' is why women make good salmon anglers, their dogged feminine persistence not allowing them to accept defeat. On more than a few occasions I have left the river fishless while my wife has taken fish. Not only this, very often the one or two she catches are the only fish of the day or week, from a beat being fished by a number of skilled male anglers. Persistent is not the word, she simply will not give up, and will fish with total commitment regardless of whether she sees fish or not. I remember a week's fishing on a Solway river when there were very few fish about, and she finished the week with four fish to my one. I gave up early most days, but she kept working away and as a result was rewarded for her efforts.

Another reason why women often 'winkle out' fish, and particularly the larger residents of a pool, is, I think, directly related to the thoroughness of their endeavours. (Some have put their success

The reward for persevering. This late October cock fish was plastered in sea-lice.

at catching large fish down to the release of female pheromones, but I don't think it is. If women always caught the most salmon, or only male salmon I could see some logic to this philosophy.) I do believe that most female anglers catch large fish because they generally work their way down a pool very much more slowly than their male counterparts, and it is this which has accounted for the downfall of the larger fish so frequently caught by them – perhaps because the larger fish need more goading than the smaller ones. When a pool is fished by a male angler the fly may pass over a fish only once or twice, whereas when fished by the opposite sex it does so a number of times and this thoroughness undoubtedly often brings success. Thus on more than one occasion when I have fished the length of a pool and wound in my line, I have turned round to see my wife still up near the top of the pool with her rod buckling under the weight of a fish.

If catching salmon depended on selecting the unique pattern, colour, style and size of fly for the prevailing conditions, then very few would ever get caught. Taking into account all the local, regional and personal variations in salmon fly design, there is such a bewilderingly large assortment to choose from that selecting the 'right' fly on any particular day would be more difficult than selecting the six winning numbers in the National Lottery two weeks running. Salmon are difficult enough to tempt at the best of times and because of this it is wrong for writers to discuss fly selection as though choosing the right one depended upon some sort of privileged divine information.

DEALING WITH TENTATIVE FISH

Regardless of what theory you follow when it comes to fly selection, there comes a time in every salmon fly fisher's life when he or she will come across a fish that continues to rise to the fly, but refuses to take hold. Before we look at how we can persuade these fish into obliging, we will consider why they should react like this.

First of all we must try and observe what a fish is doing when it rises, and establish if it has its mouth open or closed when it comes to our fly. This is not always possible, however, as very often salmon will only break the surface of the water with their dorsal fin, and some do not break the surface at all – if this is the case and if the water also happens to be turbid, you may not even know a fish has shown interest. These fish will often go undetected, unless the water is clear and we can see the occurrence, or a boil appears in the vicinity of our fly to tell us of their presence.

Salmon are as individual as those pursuing them: thus some will rise repeatedly but keeping their mouths firmly closed, while others will clearly be seen to have their mouths wide open. If we can establish whether the salmon's mouth is closed

or open at the time it rises, we can adopt suitable tactics in order to try and tempt it into making a fatal mistake: I believe a fish which rises with its mouth closed is only 'casually' interested in what is being offered, and is not excited enough by its presence to take hold; whilst a fish which rises with its mouth agape is fully intent on mouthing our offering. Thus each fish requires a different approach.

Tactics with Tentative Fish

Some past and present authorities suggest 'resting' rising fish and then trying them again with the same fly, though the amount of 'resting' time allowed seems to vary: one stated that he normally rests a fish for four or five minutes, while another said that he would go and fish another pool, only returning to try it again after an hour or so has elapsed. On returning to the fish, both said they would try it first with the original fly, and if that failed to make it respond positively, then the next manoeuvre was often to keep the same pattern, but to change down in hook size.

I remember a fish I took from the top of the Little Stream, on the Strathspey Angling Improvement Association water on 19 July 1993. As far as I can remember without checking my record book, the river on this occasion was running with an additional 8in (20cm) on the gauge. Most anglers visiting the river and fishing the pool seem to prefer fishing from the right-hand bank; my own preference, however, and that of the locals, is do so from the left because there is a nice, albeit short section of streamy water a short distance out which can be covered easily from this bank. On the far side of the stream there are one or two boulders which break and ruffle the surface. On the first time down the stream a neb, fin and tail appeared very close to my fly, a Silver Stoat tied on a size 8 Esmond Drury. I was certain it had taken my fly, but it hadn't, and the end of my line did not slide away beneath the waves as I was expecting. I tried it again, but it did not show.

I then fished all the way down to the head stream of Tarric Mor. There was a good run of fish coming through, but I had no further offers as I fished down. On returning to the top of the pool I changed down to a size 10, and in exactly the same place as before my silver teaser rolled over my fly again. To cut a long story short, on the third time down the pool I changed down to a size 12 and as my fly came round to the same place where the fish had moved to my offering twice before, my anticipation was rewarded. After a short struggle it went belly up and I tailed it out.

William Scrope in his book *Days and Nights of Salmon Fishing* wrote about tempting fish which rose to the fly without taking hold. The approach advocated was this: if he rose a fish to a Lady of Mertoun, he would rest it and change to a Toppy. He discoursed that this course of change, and vice versa, would produce fish with 'certainty'. If this was indeed the case, I would like to see what both these flies look like. Having read a great deal by past and present authoritative authors on salmon fishing, I have yet to come across any who give satisfactory reason, as far as I am concerned, as to why a reduction in fly size is often successful. More often than not the reason given is that the 'wrong' size fly was selected in the first place. In fact we don't actually know why a salmon takes a lure when it returns to freshwater, but the fact that it will refuse one fly and yet quite

confidently take a smaller one provides scope for many questions.

To my mind, if a salmon rises to a fly and refuses it, it means that it is more than just a little interested in what is being offered. Some anglers will give these fish a few casts, and if they don't take what is being presented, will give them 'best' and move on down the pool. However, these salmon are active, interested fish, which means they are potential takers and should be addressed further; after all, the majority of salmon when they return to freshwater usually ignore everything shown to them. When this sort of thing happens I am inclined to think that something other than 'size' is putting the fish off from making the final commitment. My own theory is that by scaling down the lure, the current through the lie allows the fibres incorporated within the dressing to be manipulated more easily by the prevailing stream. As far as I am concerned a fly tied on a size 10 is bound to behave in a much more enticing manner than one tied on a size 8 or 6, because it will be given more life, even when the same pattern is used in each case. Perhaps in the larger fly the current acting on the stiffer fibres making up the dressing is not vitalized enough to provoke a response.

When a fish rises to a fly with its mouth agape I believe its intention is to take hold of it. I also believe that when this mouth-agape behaviour occurs either the fly is being fished too close to the surface, or it has a focusing problem. If the fly is fished very close to the surface its overall size will effectively double, because the 'real' fly and its reflected image will appear eyelet to eyelet, and as a result, both flies will appear as the one entity to the fish. A focusing handicap may not be a problem when attacking shoals of krill or shrimp, but when targeting individual items it will be. No doubt some will regard this as nonsense: perhaps it is, but like every other animal on this planet, salmon can suffer from eye deficiencies and irregularities too.

Another reason why a fish might miss a fly could be that the prevailing light at the time was causing a surface sparkle, especially if it was sunny and the water surface well broken. Anybody who has fished for Atlantic salmon regularly with the dry fly in Alaska or the Kola Peninsula in Russia will know that on many occasions fish will be seen to rise mouth agape, giving every indication they are going to engulf it, but then for some reason miss it. I have noticed that the fish most likely to behave in such a manner are grilse, along with the occasional larger summer salmon, when presented with a smallish subsurface fly fished with a floating line. Generally one sees a lovely languid head and tail rise, the salmon's mouth is open, and you await the line jumping to life as the fish goes down with the fly – and then nothing happens.

On experiencing this particular behaviour when using a floating line and small fly fished close to the surface, I will stay where I am and cover the fish a few more times with the same fly. If this does not produce a positive response I will initially change the angle of presentation; this I have found on occasions brings more success than just changing down. Having changed my angle of presentation to no avail, I will next change to a heavier fly. If fishing with a fly tied on a double hook, I will change to one tied on a treble of the same size, or if I think conditions justify it, I will exchange it for a small Waddington shank, or a small tube fly tied on either an aluminium, copper, or brass tube. My choice will depend on three

things: the speed of the current, the water height, and the depth at which I wish to present my new offering. Now and again a heavier fly does not produce the desired effect and on occasions I have had to change my fly line to one having a higher density. I recall one fish which rose repeatedly to a fly I was presenting with a floater: having tried a different angle of presentation and heavier flies to no avail, I changed my floating line to one having an intermediate density. It was only when I changed lines for a fourth time to a fast sinker that the fish took.

When fishing with medium- and fast-sinking lines when hunting these fish I have found it unproductive to use copper or brass tubes, but have found it is best to stick to either the original fly or one of similar size tied on a Waddington shank or aluminium tube. On more than one occasion such a policy has resulted in fish which I don't think I would have taken had I stuck with my original tactics. One interesting thing that I have noticed with these fish is that, when presented with a heavier fly fishing only slightly deeper in the water, they did not break the surface when they rose to it, something they did previously.

An alternative method used by some anglers for fish which come time and again to a fly without taking hold is to change their fly to one of a different colour. To be honest I do not see any logic in this approach, especially if the new fly is going to be fished at the same depth. If we look at the fish in question – that is, those that rise with a slow nose and tail through the surface – I do not see a change of colour making any difference. The reason for this is that if the fly is being fished just subsurface, the fish will not be able to detect any colour anyway as the fly will be appearing in silhouette against the light background of the sky. If, on the other hand, a fish comes repeatedly to a deep-sunk fly without taking hold, then I am ready to accept that a change of colour could possibly provide the necessary additional stimulus to make the fish take. However, this theory only holds water if the salmon's optics allow it to detect colour. Scientific research makes me believe they can. I also believe that if a fly is fished deep, or is viewed at eye level either from behind or side on, then a change of colour could well make all the difference. Hugh Falkus in his book *Salmon Fishing – A Practical Guide* wrote:

> Who can say that at some time or other a flash of jungle cock cheek or a gleam of gold ribbing on a fly has not induced a fish to seize it ? ... There is, however, an important proviso: fly-changing should never become a fetish, for this results in 'fly-twitch' – a disease whose consequences, although unsuspected, are none-the-less unfortunate. Sooner or later an angler suffering from this miserable affliction – never content for long with any pattern he chooses, and constantly wading ashore to fiddle with his scissors and fly case – will miss the chance of a taking fish. This particular salmon, resting briefly on its way up-river, has moved on again by the time our hero has completed yet another change of fly and returned to the fray.

Detecting Tentative Fish

The main problem with fish that come to a deeply sunk fly is detecting them. In my experience they will very often only come to a fly once, and they are far less inclined to indulge in the same eccentric behaviour as their surface 'teasing' counterparts. Very often any 'deep' activity goes unnoticed by the angler, who progresses on down the pool oblivious to what is happening. On occasions fish will rise off the bottom, show interest in a fly the first time it is covered, and ignore it every other time.

One method I read about in the August 1992 edition of the *Trout & Salmon* magazine described a truly innovative technique to overcome these fish, based on using a fly dressed with a different wing colour on each side. Zsigmond Kovacs wrote the article, and described how he and friends when fishing the Morrum river in Sweden had watched the reaction of a fish that would rise to a fly on the first cast, balance it on the end of its nose, and then sink back to its lie without taking hold; when offered the same fly for a second time, it would ignore it completely. Observing this behaviour, Kovacs was inspired to come up with a fly that would show the fish two 'firsts': thus it is shown the darkest or drabbest side first, then the fly swings round past it,changing colour right in front of its nose. For obvious reasons, these flies are called Chameleon. The purpose of Kovacs' invention was to keep the salmon's interest without having to change flies – he hoped that seeing the fly change from one colour to another so quickly would provoke the fish into a positive response. Kovacs recommended using solid, or stiff winging material; however, I have found that laying two contrasting colours of bucktail side by side on each side of the shank seems to produce the necessary colour change as far as the fish are concerned.

In order to present these flies correctly from both banks it is necessary to have some with the 'bright' colour on opposite sides of the shank. For instance, suppose we are going to fish from the right bank facing downstream with the current flowing from left to right: the fly fished in this case would need to have the drab colour swimming towards the bank on which we are fishing from – in other words, looking from the front of the hook, the drab colour should be on the right-hand side of the shank. If, on the other hand, we are fishing from the left-hand bank, then the drab colour should be tied on the left-hand side. By choosing the correct dressing for the bank from which we are fishing, we will be showing the fish the dull side first, and then the coloured. If all this sounds too complicated to remember, then just think 'dull angler', meaning that the dull side of the fly – regardless of which way the current is flowing, or which bank you are fishing from – should always be swinging towards the angler.

If a change of fly brings about renewed enthusiasm, then change it; however, don't start changing for change's sake. All this does is keep your fly out of the water.

Tempting 'Difficult' Fish

Whenever I come across an interested 'difficult' fish – one which rises once and keeps its mouth closed – I will initially change my fly in order to try and persuade it to respond more positively. I will not change it for a smaller version of the same pattern, but prefer instead to change it for a different style, one which the current will give greater essence to when I swim it through the lie. If a fish rises to a standard bucktail pattern I will replace it with something which is completely different, perhaps a Strip Wing type such as a Carron or Lady Caroline, traditional Spey-type flies. In that they have an accumulation of fine, highly mobile Heron fibres, these flies are a perfect choice for streamy water – it was, after all, on streamy rivers that both these patterns originated. Scaled down to sizes 12, 10, and 8, I find they work very well. Although the originals were tied on single hooks, I prefer mine tied on Partridge Low Water doubles. Sometimes I have found that it works well to put on something ridiculously long such as an Ally's Shrimp with an extra long tail, then to cast it square across and strip it back quickly.

Another method I will try is to 'blitz' the fish, an approach I also use when fishing for trout which rise eagerly to natural flies while refusing every artificial presented. Some years ago when I was still in my teens I spent a great deal of time fishing the dry fly for trout. One small section of my local water held some good specimens, but it was quite difficult to fish, having overhanging branches in places which came right down to the water's surface. As well as this, the water was full of boils and eddies which made the elimination of drag a problem. The trout which resided here were very well educated and as a result seldom succumbed. One day I misjudged my cast and it landed in among the foliage. Gently pulling in line it fell off, landed with a plop and was whipped away instantaneously with the current – and to my surprise, a fish rose and grabbed it! After this I deliberately employed this tactic with good success. I later found by a similar casting mistake that a fly landing and fishing as I previously described can provoke salmon into taking as well.

Since my first episode with a salmon I have modified the technique a little, in that I no longer use the foliage on the opposite bank. I also present a heavier, longer fly above the fish so it lands with a decided splash, and then I strip it in quickly as soon as it lands. In order to present the fly properly with this approach, the cast should be made above and square to the fish. For whatever reason, salmon which have continually risen to a conventionally fished fly, will very often 'take' the first time they are covered when fished for in this fashion. I have also from time to time hooked salmon on a Devon Minnow as soon as this has splashed down.

Why salmon react positively to a lure which splashes the surface I am not sure; however, I am inclined to think it could possibly be something to do with the sudden and abrupt intrusion of territory within the lie. If these tactics don't work I will wind in my line, utter a quiet curse and move on.

Catching Fresh Fish

On occasions my wife and I are able to fish the first freshwater holding pools on a small spate stream. The fish which enter this lower section of the river are extremely fresh – but are no easier to catch than they would be if they were 20 miles (32km) upstream. While fishing these lower pools for the first time a few years back, my wife and I experienced the most frustrating few days' fishing we have ever had. It was the end of July, and needless to say the weather did not favour well for salmon fishing, with bright cloudless skies and low water conditions. If we were fishing anywhere else on the river I don't think we would have bothered to wet a line, but with the beat in question being so close to the sea and having the reputation for producing good sport at this time of the year, we couldn't resist having a go.

However, we found that although very fresh, the fish would rise to our flies, but would turn away at the last minute. These fish would rise whenever we presented them with a fly, but refused everything regardless of how we presented it; some had their mouths clearly open, while others kept them firmly closed. We tried all sorts of 'tricks' to provoke a positive response. On the last day I managed to hook a fish only to have it come off after a few seconds. This fish took a tiny fly that was fishing close enough to the surface for me to see it producing a small wake.

At the time I thought no more of it, but a few weeks later we were fishing another river and during lunch this strange salmon behaviour came up in conversation. One of the other anglers had regularly taken the lowest beat on another river for a number of years, fishing it at the same time of year, the end of July, and he had experienced what I previously described. As it transpired he eventually got talking to the local expert who had regular access to the stretch when no one else was fishing it! He was told that in order to catch the fish in these lower pools the fly had to be 'in' the surface film as it traversed across the stream. If it was entirely on or below the surface, the fish for some reason continued to show interest, but would not take hold. When I heard this my mind instantly returned to the fish that I hooked momentarily. Perhaps this was the answer, because on reflection my fly at the time when the fish took it, may well have been in this transitory position. The reason given by the local doyen for a fly being taken while fished in this position, but refused when on or below the surface, was due to the salmon's eyesight having not yet adapted to the less saline environment. He explained that a fly which pierced the surface tension film would be much more conspicuous to the salmon than it would if it appeared down in the water.

Since this goes contrary to what I have experienced and described earlier in this book, I am inclined to dismiss this explanation. However, the next time I fished the beat I gave some time to his idea. I attached a small polystyrene ball to the front of a small Stoat's Tail which was tied on a low water single hook in order to try and deliver the fly as he prescribed. Although the fly worked, it did not deliver outstanding sport, perhaps because I was not fishing it in quite the right way. So far I have taken one fish on it. Most of the fish which I and my wife have taken to date from the beat we fish have fallen to Ally's Shrimp of varying sizes, stripped back quickly beneath the surface. The only reason I can extend regarding the different success rates of the same method in the two rivers is that the section fished by the other angler is tidal, whereas ours, although close to the sea, is not. Whether this is in fact the reason I don't know.

4 NEW WAYS WITH WADDINGTONS AND TUBES

Before looking at some of the modern techniques employed with these shanks I think it is best to take a look at what they are, and how they came into existence. The Waddington fly in its simplest form is a dressed steel shank with an eye at the front to which the nylon is tied, and an eye at the rear for the fastening of a treble hook. Early patterns were dressed with heron hackles, and gave a very sleek, streamlined appearance when pulled through the water. However, heron hackles are soft and cannot stand a lot of punishment, and so modern patterns are almost exclusively tied using bucktail. Nevertheless the original flies which were tied with heron hackle had a semblance in the water that many of the modern hairwing patterns lack. A few of the 'better' tackle shops still occasionally sell Waddington shanks tied with heron hackles, and if you know of such a place I would recommend purchasing a few. Alternatively you could always attempt tying some yourself, or inquire of the many professional tiers who advertise in the monthly magazines as to whether you could commission them to tie some for you.

HOW THE WADDINGTON FLY EVOLVED

Richard Waddington was the inventor of the shank, and he persuaded Alexander Martin of Glasgow to manufacture them. During March of 1950 he received the first batch. The flies were then used during April and May, and the result was fifty-five fish killed, with a further five fish lost. Before he developed these flies, Richard Waddington had been looking for a 'better' lure than the 'traditionally dressed' salmon fly which was used at the time. He wanted something that would swim in the proper plane, resemble the shape of a small fish regardless of the angle from which it was viewed, and have superior hooking power. At first it was thought that the front end of the shanks would need to be made heavier than the rear, though later it was discovered that in actual fact this would not be necessary, as the flies remained horizontal. It was also believed that the treble hook at the rear created drag, thus causing the tail to lift. I agree that the treble hook does provide lift due to its shape and surface area, but in saying this, modern manufactured shanks for one reason or another have an annoying tendency to swim tail down. Whether this is due to variances between the original and the modern double-shanked versions, I don't know. Later in the chapter I will discuss how the tail-down effect can be minimized when fishing with the double-shanked variety.

The original Waddington shank consisted of a single trunk and was constructed with a slight rear taper. This meant that the end to which the hook was attached was thicker and heavier than the front, where the nylon was tied. The later version, the black-japanned double-shanked Waddington, is very similar in design to the Brora shank made from stainless-steel wire and developed and popularized by Rob Wilson. At first the Brora shanks were constructed on three different gauges of wire, but since the mid- to late 70s only one gauge of 0.06in (1.5mm) wire is used. By using this gauge the hook-end eyelet of the shank can be left open for hook replacement. One other difference between the Brora and Waddington shanks is that the Broras do not have an upturned front eye. Of the two styles available, it is the black-japanned Waddington shank which has become the favoured type among the majority of modern salmon anglers. Nevertheless, these mass-produced shanks lack the weight of the Broras, which is often essential for early spring fishing.

Its Construction

The Waddington versions, like the Broras, are constructed from a single length of wire bent along itself; where it bends, eyelets are formed for the attachment of the hook and nylon. The eyelet to which the nylon is attached is completely closed, but the rear-most eyelet is left open in order to facilitate the attachment of the hook. Some anglers make their own shanks by bending wire around two nails hammered into a piece of wood with a pair of pliers. If tempted to make your own do not use copper wire, because this can easily fracture and break when playing a fish. If this occurs, the

hooks and the rear-most section of the shank will be left in the salmon's mouth. Stainless-steel wire of the type used by dental technicians is by far the best.

Its Advantages

What advantages does the modern, double-shanked Waddington offer late twentieth-century salmon anglers? Well, to start with, flies tied on them have a profile which is much slimmer compared to one of the same pattern tied on a tube. A fly tied on a tube presents a very bold image to a fish, whereas the Waddington's slimmer body allows more light through from the upper hairs of the wing, and this plays on the hairs nearest the shank on the underside; as a result these flies appear much more appealing to fish. This additional light filtration – so essential to enhance the colours of the under-wing – cannot occur with a tube because of its thicker body.

For best effect when tying Waddington-shanked flies it is essential to keep the wing material rather sparse. This has two very desirable effects: first, it allows the maximum amount of light to filter through; and second, it enables them to sink more quickly and get down to deep-lying fish, especially helpful in the cold waters of early spring and late autumn. A fly with a heavily dressed wing creates much more lift, and if it is held against the current it will swim higher in the water compared to a sparsely dressed one of similar size held in a similar flow. Depth therefore is much more difficult to achieve with a heavily dressed fly.

Another reason why the Waddington shank should be included in the armoury of any serious salmon angler's tackle is because they are much easier and safer to cast, largely because they are not constantly trying to part company from the end of the leader, unlike their brass or copper tube equivalents. This is not to say that I don't like using tubes, because I do, I use them regularly, especially when the water is very cold and the fish are lying 'doggo' on the bottom, or when rivers are running high and coloured. Both Waddingtons and tubes have their own unique qualities, and both will produce the desired results – i.e. the interests of a fish – but to do so they must be fished in different ways and at different times.

Its Disadvantages

Although the Waddington shank has many followers, there are still a great many anglers who don't like using them, preferring a tube or a long-shanked treble such as the Partridge X3, the Kamasan B380 or the Mustad 80550BLs instead. Having

talked to a number of these anglers, it transpires that there are two main reasons why they dislike them: one concerns initial attachment of the treble hook, and the other – which seems to be the main aversion for many – appears to be with the removal and replacement of broken hooks. Even so, I have to say that by neglecting these shanks they are denying themselves a superb means of attracting and killing fish, because flies tied on Waddington shanks have an agility and presence in the water that they would never have with tubes.

HOOK SELECTION

When it comes to selecting hooks for their shanks, far too many anglers use trebles which are either too small, too large, or over-heavy. If the hook is on the small side it will not have the same opportunities to

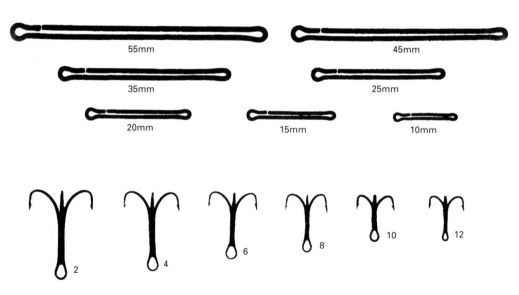

Fig 3 Partridge VIB Waddington Shanks and Partridge XIB Trebles.

secure a hold, especially if the mouth of the fish does not close properly around it. On the other hand, if the hook is over large the fly will swim in a 'tail down' fashion, and although this probably does not affect its hooking ability, the fly's mobility and attractiveness is greatly reduced, which results – needless to say – in fewer offers. In Table 3 I have listed the type and size of treble hooks I recommend when using Partridge V1B Waddington shanks in lengths ranging from ⅜ to 2¼in (10 to 55mm); *see* also Fig 3. All Partridge Waddington shanks V1B and Partridge outpoint treble X1B hooks shown in Fig 3 are actual size.

It should be noted that the overall length of each shank will in fact be longer than the lengths given in Table 3: this is because the length given by Partridge for their V1Bs only corresponds to the part of the shank to which the dressing of the fly is applied, i.e. the 2¼in (55mm) shank in the table has a total length of 2¾in (70mm). In addition the hook when attached will also add significantly to the overall length of the fly: thus in the same example given of a 2¼in (55mm) shank, the fly length will be closer to 4in (100mm) when tied (this is assuming that a size 2 Partridge X1 type treble is used, and that the hair extends beyond the bends by at least ¼in (6mm). So when buying shanks to tie up into flies, the difference between the stated length and the actual length must be taken into consideration.

I prefer these hooks on the end of my Waddingtons because they are lighter in weight compared to the other types available. Although I like the Partridge Rob Wilson CS9 outpoint trebles when fishing with tubes, as far as I am concerned they are, size for size, a little on the heavy side for fishing with a lightweight shank compared with the X1 trebles. I must say, however, that the Partridge X1 hooks are purely a personal preference, and I have a number of friends who use the CS9 on their own Waddingtons to good effect. Whichever of the two hooks you choose, both are excellent and have exceptional hooking qualities.

ATTACHING HOOKS

Hooks can be attached in a variety of ways. Some anglers I know fit the hook before putting on the dressing, while others prefer to wait until the dressing has been completed. The main problem with the first of these methods is that the hook points get in the way when dressing the shank, besides endangering the fingers; be particularly careful when laying down the initial turns of tying thread onto the shank, or when finishing off the head, as this is when most accidents seem to occur – usually because they are done at speed. I have seen more than one experienced fly dresser give themselves a nasty cut by being in too much of a rush. Another drawback with

Waddington Length Partridge V1B	Recommended Partridge X1 Trebles
⅜in (10mm)	12
½in (12.5mm)	12, 10
⅝in (15mm)	12, 10, 8
¾in (20mm)	12, 10, 8, 6
1in (25mm)	10, 8, 6, 4
1⅜in (35mm)	10, 8, 6, 4, 2
1¾in (45mm)	10, 8, 6, 4, 2
2¼in (55mm)	8, 6, 4, 2

Table 3.

this method is that all too often the dressing is taken down over the rear eyelet of the shank, and in this instance a damaged hook cannot be replaced without spoiling the dressing of the fly; very often the shank has to be stripped, and a new fly tied after the replacement hook has been connected.

Alternatively you can wait and attach the hook after the dressing has been finished. With this approach the dressing must be completed a little distance in front of the rear eyelet, otherwise the hook cannot be fitted in the conventional fashion. If you decide to dress the shank first, the rear eyelet must remain clear of the dressing so the hook can be attached conventionally; in which case, take care not to damage the wings when securing it.

As we have already said, when it comes to attaching hooks a variety of techniques may be used.

Method One: Whipping with Nylon
Secure a small length, usually about 1in (25mm), of heavy breaking-strain nylon –

20lb – to the shank of the treble with tying thread. In order to add extra colour to the fly, some anglers and fly dressers will use a coloured tying thread for this purpose. When whipping the nylon to the hook shank, approximately ⅝in (15mm) of nylon should be left projecting forward of the eye of the hook when you are finished. The rear hook-fastening eyelet of the shank should then be opened slightly so the hook's eyelet can pass through easily; once this has been done, it should be closed with a pair of small, long-nosed pliers. Some anglers will then bind the closed rear eyelet on the shank with either thin copper wire or tying thread to prevent it from opening out when playing a fish, though to be honest I don't think this is necessary if the eyelet has been closed properly. The remaining length of nylon protruding forward of the hook is now laid along the body of the shank and secured with tying thread; this will stop the treble hook from hinging away from the horizontal plane when the fly is being fished (*see* Fig 4).

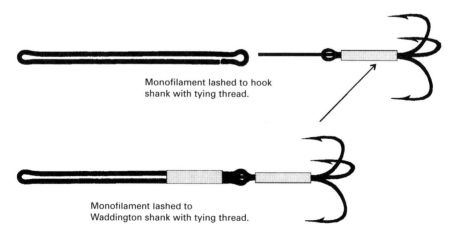

Monofilament lashed to hook shank with tying thread.

Monofilament lashed to Waddington shank with tying thread.

Fig 4 Keeping the hook 'true' on a Waddington shank by using a length of stout nylon.

Method Two: Using Heat Shrink Tubing

A more up-to-date technique employed for the same purpose is the use of heat shrink tubing. First cut a length a little longer than the shank of the treble. Now place it over the shank of the treble and pull it past the eye towards the bends of the hooks. After this, the eye of the hook is passed through the opened rear eyelet on the Waddington shank. As before, once the eyelet of the hook has been passed through the open eyelet of the shank, close it with a pair of long-nosed pliers (as described earlier, the rear eyelet on the shank can then be bound with tying thread). Once this is done, the heat shrink should be pulled back along the shank of the treble so that approximately half remains over the shank of the hook, and the other half comes over the rear hook-attaching eyelet of the Waddington. A few seconds heat applied from a domestic hair drier at a 'hot' setting is usually all that is required to complete the job. In order to achieve a good, even shrinkage, rotate the shank between your fingers while holding the nozzle of the dryer about 2in (50mm) away; once the tubing starts to show signs of shrinking, move the nozzle back and forth from one end to the other. If you are doing this to a shank which has had the dressing applied before the hook is fixed, hold the hair of the wings to one side while applying the heat, otherwise the heat from the drier will crinkle them. A word of warning: keep your fingers out of the way as well, as things can get a little warm!

One disadvantage with heat shrink tubing is that a thin film of water tends to remain between it and the shank of the treble. Hooks attached in this fashion therefore need to be 'blow-dried' at the end of a day's fishing; if you omit to do this, the next time you want to use the shanks you will find the hooks have started to corrode. Many anglers are now starting to put heat shrink tubing over the dressing on the shanks before they tie on the wings, to protect the soft floss and tinsel materials from any damage which may be inflicted by the sharp teeth of kelts and autumn kippers.

Many anglers fail to take into account when adding this tubing to their flies that heat shrink tubing is a relatively heavy material, and even in short lengths it will increase a fly's overall weight. A length of clear standard heat shrink tubing used to cover a 2¼in (55mm) shank could add anything from 5 to 10 per cent more weight (depending on the make of the tubing) to the overall weight of an undressed shank. As when used to hold the hook in line with the shanks, the ends of the tubing are never completely sealed and as a result water seepage will occur; this is because the heat shrink will only reduce in size to the highest spot onto which it is being heated. Water infiltrates between the dressing and the tubing, and as a result the body dressing of flies protected in such a fashion will always remain wet. These flies are also heavier to cast and fish with than a shank that does not have heat shrink fitted, because the water cannot be thrown off during the back and forward casts as it would with a standard, 'unprotected' shank, and saturates the body material of the dressing. As a result these flies therefore also tend to fish slightly deeper in the water.

If conventional heat shrink tubing is used to protect the body dressing of the fly, the two ends of the heat shrink once shrunk into place should be sealed with a thin coat of varnish or Super Glue. Contrary to what many people believe, standard conventional heat shrink tubing does not provide a watertight seal, so if you are determined to use it for covering body materials then I would recommend the type that has an internal adhesive. The current price for adhesive-lined, heat shrink tubing ranges from £8 to £12 per metre and can be obtained from most good electrical trade counters.

One thing to look out for when purchasing this type of tubing is that some cheaper makes look transparent prior to heating, but once treated they turn foggy. If the tubing loses its clarity, the colour of the body floss will be misrepresented, while the sparkle and flash given off from the tinsel ribbing may be greatly reduced. To avoid these problems, ask the sales person about the tubing's post-shrink characteristics prior to purchasing. As well as transparent, heat shrink tubing is available in black, green, red, yellow and yellow/ green. Many anglers who tie their own flies are now starting to use this coloured tubing as a means of providing a quick body dressing. Before shrinking the tubing around the shank, they tie in the tinsel of their choice so that it can be wound over the tubing after it has been shrunk into place.

Some anglers will then finish off the fly by encapsulating the body tubing and tinsel rib with a clear adhesive heat shrink. If an over-wide oval tinsel is employed on these shanks the body starts to look like an emaciated corkscrew: this is because the heat shrink when stretched tight over the tinsel exaggerates the spiralling of the rib. A number of anglers I know who tie and fish flies tied in this fashion swear they have superior action in the water to traditionally dressed shanks. From what I have observed, not only do these corkscrew-bodied flies rise and fall as they are buffeted by the current as they swim across pools, but they wobble gently from side to side too, as the water screws its way along the ribbing of the shank. And the wider the oval tinsel, the greater the wobble!

Method Three: Using Silicone Rubber Tubing

Another method of attaching a hook, similar to the previous method, is to use a length of silicone rubber tubing. This is positioned over the shank of the treble hook and shank in the same way as the heat shrink tubing, although no heat is needed to complete the task. Unlike the heat shrink, the silicone rubber tubing is not so tight-fitting and therefore any water that has ingressed between the shank and tubing can run out. Hooks attached with the silicone-type tubing are 'aired' more easily, meaning they are less prone to rusting, especially if put back into the fly box wet.

To provide a 'straight' hook when using silicone rubber tubing, I recommend using some that has a slightly smaller inside diameter than the outside diameter of the smallest of the two eyelets; this gives a snugger fit around the hook shank and keeps it from moving about when being fished. For those who like the hook to 'hinge' back and forth when playing fish, I would recommend using either the lashed nylon method, or this one. If, on the other hand, you like the hook to remain straight in line with the shank, the heat shrink permits the minimum possible movement; of the two methods so far described of attaching and securing a treble to a Waddington shank, this is the one I would use because I feel that the minimum amount of lateral movement a hook has, the better the hold it will establish and the less chance there is of the hooks fouling the leader when being cast. When I used silicone rubber to keep the hook straight, I found the hooks would on occasions get caught up around the leader, particularly when casting against a strong wind. The reason for this I think was due to the silicone tubing flexing and allowing the hooks to pivot out of position.

I remember one occasion on the Doon when there was a strong upstream wind blowing when I was fishing a large orange hairwing fly tied on a 2¼in (55mm) Waddington shank above a small weir during a spate. The river was experiencing an exceptional run of fish, and there was a steady stream of salmon coming over the dam I was fishing above. Needless to say I thought it only a matter of time before one would introduce itself to my fly. To cut a long story short, I had two fish take my fly, flurry the surface when I raised the rod – and then fall off. On inspecting my fly after

each incident I noticed the hooks had caught around the leader. As a result I concluded my fly was fishing back to front when both fish took hold. What was a little annoying about the experience was that the other four rods fishing at the time finished the day with over twenty fish between them. The two I 'lost' were the only two fish I touched all day. One consolation, however, was that all the other rods were spinning at the time, and even to have hooked and lost two on the fly, I experienced what can only be recorded as 'one-upmanship'. Since I have started to use heat shrink tubing to keep the hooks straight I have not experienced them catching on the leader to the same extent. For fitting the silicone and heat shrink tubing, *see* Fig 5.

Method Four: Using Amalgamating Tape

One new innovative method of keeping the hook in line with the shank is by using

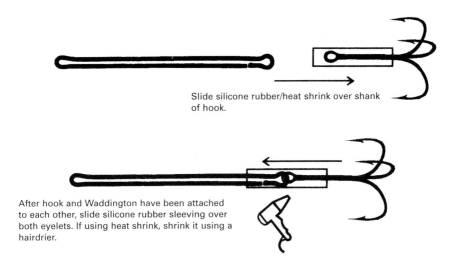

Slide silicone rubber/heat shrink over shank of hook.

After hook and Waddington have been attached to each other, slide silicone rubber sleeving over both eyelets. If using heat shrink, shrink it using a hairdrier.

Fig 5 Keeping the hook 'true' on a Waddington shank by means of silicone rubber and heat-shrink tubing.

amalgamating or self-annealing tape. This tape is totally waterproof and adheres to itself when stretched. In order to use the tape with these flies the shank needs to be dressed short so as to leave the rear eyelet clear for fitting the hook. The eyelet is opened slightly to allow the eye of the hook to pass through, and then closed with a pair of long-nosed pliers as described previously. Once this has been done, cut a short length of ¾in (20mm) wide tape. Apply half its width over the undressed section of the shank and the other half over the front section of the hook. Now stretching the tape, put three or four turns around both the shank of the hook and the Waddington.

By using this tape, broken hooks can be changed simply and easily because all one has to do is unwind the tape, open the rear eyelet, change the broken hook, close the eyelet and rebind with a fresh piece of tape. Like heat shrink tubing, this tape also comes in various colours, all of which can be used to add a little extra colour to a fly – which, who knows, on the day may well make all the difference!

Method Five: 'Through the Eyes'

Although I have used all the methods described, I prefer the one which I am now going to explain. Earlier I mentioned that the principal dislike that many anglers have towards these shanks is the difficulty of replacing broken hooks, especially on the river bank. A method which I helped develop, and which I call 'through the eyes', works very well. This method of attaching a replacement hook is very similar to how you would connect a treble hook to a tube. First remove the damaged hook from the shank and then select a suitable length of silicone rubber tubing. For a Waddington of 2in (50mm) use a piece about ¾in (20mm) long. Now take the nylon and feed it through the front eyelet on the Waddington shank from the top side. Once this has been done, thread the nylon through the rear eyelet from the bottom side and then feed it through the length of silicone rubber tubing (the length and internal diameter of the tubing will depend on the length of the shank being used). Pull about 12in (30cm) of the nylon through the tubing. This makes tying the treble hook easy. Now tie the treble onto the nylon with a tucked half-blood knot. Once the hook has been tied to the nylon push the front half of the hook about half way into the tubing. Now push the remaining tubing over the rear of the shank by about ½in (12mm). Finally lie the nylon along the underside of the shank.

An alternative approach is to bring the nylon through the front eyelet from the bottom and feed it through the rear eyelet from the top. This way it lies along the top of the shank. Whether the nylon is threaded through the front eyelet from the top or bottom side depends mainly on where and how I am going to fish the fly. When fishing a strong, deep flow with a medium to fast sinking line I like to feed the nylon through the front eyelet of the shank from the top. This helps to keep the fly swimming in the horizontal plane, because the front upturned eyelet on the shank acts as a hydro-vane; the more acute the upturned angle, the greater the amount of lift it will achieve. I have a few shanks in my box to which I have taken a pair of pliers and increased the angle on the front eyelet. These I particularly like to use when fishing slow featureless flows when hand lining with a medium to fast sinking line: when fished with a pull-and-pause action

Fishing the River Tarff. Even on rivers as small as this one, a double-handed fly rod would be my first choice during a spate.

these modified shanks fish with a rise-and-dive action as they are pulled through the water. However, I might add that they are of little use when fished with a floating line when there is any semblance of a flow, because they skate.

If fishing a medium-paced current and I find I have only a floating line available, I will on occasions take the fly off and turn it over, especially if I feel my flies are not fishing deep enough, or if I want to fish a large lightweight, mobile fly fast, just under the surface. Having taken it off, the eyelet will now be facing downwards. Next I pass the nylon through the eyelet from what is normally the bottom side of the shank. By performing this simple change, any water pressure acting on the down-facing eyelet causes the fly to be pushed downwards. I acknowledge the downward force exerted will not be great,

even in a fast flow, but sometimes it is enough to stop the fly from skating. Not only can we increase the fly's versatility by threading the nylon through the front eyelet, this arrangement is also an excellent way of using Waddington shanks that have their hook-attaching eyelets broken; the only difference is that the nylon cannot be passed through the rear eyelet on the shank before passing it through the silicone rubber tubing (the nylon through the front eye arrangement can be seen in Fig 6).

Procedure for Fitting a New Hook, or Utilizing a Shank that Has the Rear Eyelet Broken

1) Remove the broken hook.
2) Slide off the old silicone rubber tubing, or heat shrink if fitted.

73

Note: if the rear eyelet on the shank is broken, start at stage 3.

3) Pass the monofilament through the front eyelet. It can be threaded through the eyelet either from the top or the bottom.
4) Now thread the monofilament through a suitable length of silicone sleeving.
5) Tie the nylon to the hook.
6) Next, push the hook approximately half-way into the sleeving.
7) Now push the sleeving along with the hook over the rear end of the shank.
8) Finally, lie the nylon snugly along the body of the shank.

Some anglers might think that a Waddington shank which has a treble attached to it in this way will be less attractive: let me assure you now, they do not lose any of their charms – if anything they become more alluring. Passing the nylon through the eyelets helps to keep the fly swimming true in the current, and stops it developing a tail-down presence, not an infrequent occurrence with Waddington shanks with a conventionally attached hook. The reason for the improvement is that the hook is now attached to the nylon direct, and so instead of being towed by the shank, the hook now effectively pushes it, in the same way as a tube, or a Devon Minnow. Let me explain further: something can only be pulled if the 'moving' force is secured at the front. The body of the Waddington shank in this case, like the body of a Devon Minnow shell and tube fly, is free to move along the line, and it is only the water pressure pushing against it from the front which keeps it in position (*see* Fig 7).

This results in the body of the shank being held in the same plane as the nylon.

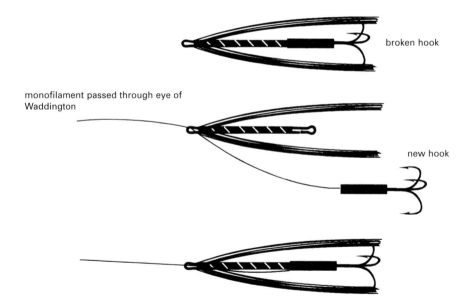

broken hook

monofilament passed through eye of Waddington

new hook

Fig 6 Through the eye connecting method for replacing a broken hook on a Waddington.

Waddington shanks that have the trebles attached using this method are better hookers and holders of fish than the ones which have the hooks fixed mechanically; this is probably because they behave like a tube in that when a fish is being played, the shank slides up the line, leaving only the treble in the salmon's mouth; as a result, fewer fish come off I think mainly due to the fact that the hook is the only object they can chew on.

Initially I only used the 'through the eyes' method as a means of attaching the hook to a favourite fly that had had its rear eyelet damaged. Nowadays, however, I keep a good quantity of the shanks in my own fly box hookless, only fastening a hook to one of them by the 'through the eyes' method when I want to fish it. This has two distinct advantages over the conventional approach: first, it saves me time when I am tying them, as I don't have to

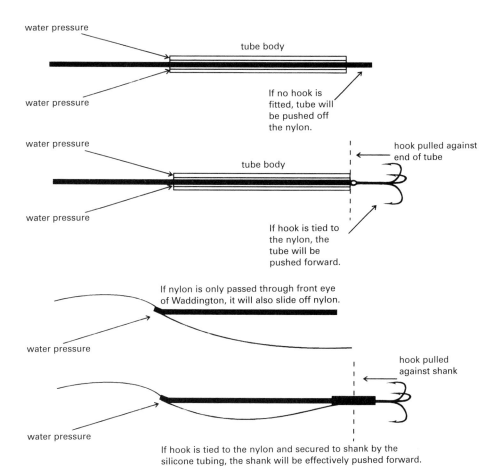

Fig 7 Diagram showing how hook effectively 'pushes' a tube and Waddington's when hook is connected through the eye.

mess about securing a hook; and second, by attaching the treble hook only just before I want to fish the fly, it saves me money, because then I don't have a large number of hooks sitting attached to a shank doing nothing. If a hook is mechanically secured to a shank it can only become employed when its fly goes for a swim; however, by waiting and connecting hooks only when they are needed, these hooks can be utilized when fishing tubes.

Although I prefer using the 'through the eyes' system of attaching hooks, I do not use it to the exclusion of all the other methods described.

TUBE FLIES

In their simplest form, a tube fly is no more than a length of plastic or metal conduit which has a bunch of hairs lashed to one end. Some tubes have a body of floss ribbed with silver or gold tinsel, although for simplicity and quickness many salmon fishers who tie their own flies frequently omit the body dressing. Interestingly, more and more anglers are tending to prefer these simple tyings. For those who like to add a sparkle to their flies, a flat or oval tinsel rib can be incorporated; where no body floss is employed it is simply spiralled along the length of the bare tube. In order to do this the tinsel is first secured to the rear of the tube by a few turns of tying thread; this is then wound along the length of the tube with five or six open spiral turns towards the head. The tinsel is then wound along the tube covering the tying silk. Some anglers will now cover the body of the tube with a length of heat shrink tubing. Although most modern hairwing patterns are reproduced in tube

form, the only *sine qua non* they have in representing the original fly is that the colour scheme is in keeping with it.

Whether you like them or not, there is no doubt that tube flies have accounted for a great many salmon since they first became readily available in the mid-1950s, the result of the mass production manufacturing techniques of metal which came about during World War II. These flies now augment many salmon anglers' fly boxes. In relation to this, plastics were finding an increasingly widespread use – until this time, flies in the form currently recognized did not exist. In fact there is very little written about the conception and production of tubes, with no one person attributed with their development. I did come across a short reference to Parker tube flies which as far as I could ascertain were made mostly from starling wing-quills, but I discovered Parker was also known to have used quills from other birds. The treble hook in these tubes was secured to a wire mount which was passed through the tube in a fashion similar to that used on a Devon Minnow; to fish them at the required depth Parker wound lead wire around the wire of the mount. Although these flies killed fish for the anglers using them, they did not catch on with the fundamentalist angling fraternity at the time.

Since the salmon close fishing season in the British Isles is very short – only three weeks, if we count Irish rivers and some Cornish rivers – it is necessary to have a selection of tubes in a wide variety of lengths and weights in order to cope with all the varied temperatures and water conditions one is likely to encounter during a long fishing season. So as to satisfy these needs, tubes are mainly manufactured in three materials, namely aluminium, brass and plastic; I tend as a rule to opt mainly for the Slipstream Fly Body type distributed by Veniard's.

Plastic Tubes

Plastic tubes come in two types, A and B, both available in lengths ranging from ½in (13mm) to 2in (50mm). Type A are made of clear plastic and have moulded ends to help prevent the dressing from coming off. In the two smaller sizes produced, the fly has a tendency to have a stocky, stout appearance. Type B plastic tubes also have moulded ends, the rearmost slightly smaller than the one at the front. There is also a small recess in the tail of the tube to allow the eyelet of the treble hook to pass through more easily. Although they appear to have a slightly smaller cross-sectional area than the type A tubes, when dressed in the two smaller sizes they too have a somewhat obese-looking appearance. When fished with a floating line in all but the slowest of flows I have found they are inclined to skate on the surface. Having said this, grilse at times will take them with alacrity, especially when fished with a neutral density line and presented just below the surface.

Both tube types are an ideal choice in the smaller lengths for fishing slow-flowing pools, especially when the water is low or warm, when a more conventional, more slimly-dressed fly tied on a double or treble hook fished close to the surface fails. In the larger sizes they are ideal when you want to present a large lightweight fly in front of a fish that will dance and dart in the water at the whim of the currents when presented with a sinking line.

Although tubes are nearly always employed as subsurface flies, the plastic type are used increasingly for surface work. As I mentioned previously, if small plastic tubes are heavily dressed they tend to be buoyant; and if fished in the standard wet fly fashion with a floating line in all but the slowest of flows, they are inclined to create a great deal of surface disturbance. Normally surface disturbance is something which should be avoided at all costs; however, there are occasions when a surface fly is the only thing which will bring fish up off the bottom. One such technique is dibbling. Due to their bulky, buoyant characteristics, small over-dressed plastic tubes are ideal as dropper flies when fishing lochs.

In the larger sizes, modified plastic tubes with long trailing wings are well suited to 'riffling', or "skating", as it is sometimes known. In order to modify a tube for this purpose, a small hole must be made in the side wall of the tube a little distance behind its head. When sliding the tube onto the nylon we do not pass it through the concentric hole running the length of the tube, we insert the nylon through the new hole instead. When the tube is cast across the stream the current pushes against the head of the tube, thus causing it to rise: as a result during its traverse of the pool it planes across the surface causing disturbance. This technique can sometimes bring up fish that have ignored small, conventionally presented subsurface flies.

Aluminium Tubes

Aluminium tubes, type C, range in sizes from ½in (13mm) to 2½in (63mm); they have a much smaller CSA (cross-sectional area) than the plastic types. They have an inner plastic liner through their length which is moulded at both ends to stop the nylon from being chaffed. Since the body of these tubes has a polished silver appearance, many anglers do not bother to incorporate a body dressing, but just tie in a few hairs at the head. In the smaller sizes these tubes are perfect for tying Silver Stoat's Tails, due to their silver finish; also, being slightly heavier than plastic tubes, size for size, they 'lie down' in the water just that little bit more and so can be fished in water which is a little above normal height and of medium pace. Because they fish deeper in the water than their plastic counterparts, aluminium tubes are a favourite choice of many anglers during those difficult changeover days which can occur in late spring and autumn.

Brass Tubes

Brass tubes, type D, come in lengths ranging from ½in (13mm) to 3in (76mm); they also have an inner plastic liner, but they do not have moulded ends to stop the dressing from coming off. So when tying these flies it is therefore advisable not to take the dressing right to the end of the tube. Size for size, these tubes are much heavier than their aluminium or plastic counterparts.

Brass tubes are mainly used during the spring and late autumn months when the water is cold. However, they are also very good for fishing heavy water lies during the summer, or for 'covering' the water when the river is carrying extra colour and height during a spate. On the River Doon, one of my local rivers, many local anglers use nothing other than a ½in (13mm) brass tube, even when the river is flowing at compensation height. One of the most popular patterns tied on these small tubes is called the Red Tube: the fly has no body dressing, only a few red bucktail hairs for a wing and two jungle cock feathers for cheeks.

When using a brass tube, regardless of its size, it is advisable to use a thicker-gauge nylon than you would for an aluminium or a plastic one. There are two reasons for this: first, a heavy tube on a narrow-gauge nylon has a tendency to behave badly; second, if a thin gauge of nylon is used with a brass tube – such as you would use when fishing with one of the other types of tube – it will stretch and fail prematurely. This could result in the tube flying off either during the forward or back cast and hitting another angler – not a very pleasant experience, I can assure you. When fishing we must always be aware not just of our own safety, but of other people's too.

Home-made Tubes

Even though the Slipstream tubes are inexpensive, some anglers prefer to make their own. When it comes to home-made plastic tubes, the refill from a ball-point pen is a firm favourite: I have used this tubing myself and found it ideal. It is relatively soft, and the treble hook can be secured simply by pushing it into it. Other sources of tubing material are the straws supplied with aerosol sprays, lollipop sticks and intravenous tubing. For those who do not wish to be seen scrounging in wastepaper bins, plastic tubing suitable for making your own flies is available from Tom C. Saville Ltd of Nottingham. They also sell 6in (15mm) lengths of plastic-lined aluminium and brass tubing which you can cut to length by using a hacksaw with a fine-toothed blade.

Why Use Tubes?

Why then should we choose to use a tube? First, because they come in various lengths and weights, and so there are very few places on a river where they cannot be put to good use. They also offer superior hooking 'potential' over conventional flies: this is because when a fish takes the fly, the tube slides clear of the treble and so the fish finds it more difficult to lever out the hook. Further, if a hook suffers any damage it can be quickly and easily replaced. However, the main advantage which tube flies have over other flies is that they can be 'queued'; this means you can create a fly of any length, colour and weight. To increase the overall length of a fly, all we do is slide the required number of tubes of similar pattern down the nylon (*see* Fig 8).

Queuing Tubes

By sliding tubes of different patterns and colours together it is possible to create countless fly variations. Moreover, yet another benefit that 'queuing' tubes has over a conventional single mounted tube is that we can create a lure of perfect weight for any flow being fished. Also by rearranging the tubes we can alter the angle at which it will swim. One problem that often arises when fishing a largish lightweight plastic tube with a floating line is the annoying habit of it fishing nose high, in other words, tail down. However, by using a 'queued tube' this problem can

easily be overcome because by placing the heaviest tube up front, nearest to the fly line, we can counteract the problem of nose lift. Likewise, if the nose of the fly is pulled down by a sinking line, a heavier tube can be placed rearmost, next to the hook, to compensate for the downward pull of the fly line.

This concept can be taken further by coupling a brass or copper tube at the front next to an aluminium or plastic one at the rear within a shroud of heat shrink tubing. The advantage of this method is that a number of tail-heavy or head-heavy compensated tubes can be manufactured before we go fishing; by doing this we have a selection of flies suitable for a wide assortment of water conditions. Anglers who exercise the previously cited practice generally tend to buy, or tie their tubes only in the smaller sizes.

Some anglers might fear that a 'lure' consisting of two or more tubes will be difficult to cast. This is not so: these flies are no more difficult to cast or control than a fly of equal length tied on a single tube. And since the fly is now effectively jointed where the tubes come together, it has greater mobility than a 'one-tube' fly of similar length because it is much more flexible. This increase in flexibility means that any incident current acting along its length will create more life in it than it

tube pushed along nylon

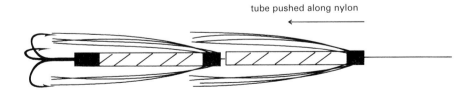

Fig 8 Queued tube assembly.

Expatiating tactics on the banks of the Tay.

would if it were acting on a mono-tube fly; thus these lures will often attract fish which have ignored a conventional tube. The one disadvantage when using a series of 'queued' tubes is that if the treble becomes caught up on some submerged nasty you will lose not one tube, but two or three.

The Dog-leg Tube

It is well known that anything which moves in an idiosyncratic fashion through the water will attract the attention of fish: this is evidenced by the interest an injured or sickly fish provokes in other larger fish. If we can therefore create in a lure the wobbling action similar to that seen in a poorly fish, we will stand a better chance of awaking the salmon's regnant predatory instinct: one fly known as the 'Dog-leg Tube' seems to do just that (*see* Fig 9).

To make a 'Dog-leg Tube' a plastic-lined aluminium or brass tube 1½in (40mm) to 3in (76mm) is required. The

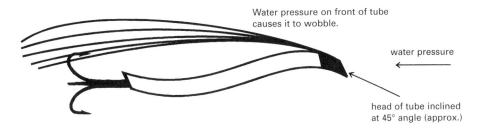

Water pressure on front of tube causes it to wobble.

water pressure

head of tube inclined at 45° angle (approx.)

Fig 9 Dog-leg Tube fly.

first step is to remove the plastic liner by cutting it at one end with either a razor blade or a scalpel. Now, to form the front of the tube, cut or file away at it until it acquires an angle of 45 degrees: this angled shape acts like a hydro-vane and will help to induce wobble. Once this has been done, remove any burrs or sharp edges that remain.

Next, using two pairs of pliers, put two bends into the tube, one about a third of the way from the front of the tube, and the other a third of the way from the rear. The front bend should be made in an upward direction, while the rear bend is made downwards. Be careful not to bend the tube too much as it will fracture. In order to stop the jaws of the pliers scratching the surface of the tube, wrap masking tape or electrical tape around the section being bent; alternatively, use a soft cloth between the jaws of the pliers and tube. The plastic liner is now inserted back into the tube and trimmed to match. In order to stop the liner from coming out, secure it by applying a small drop of Super-Glue.

For simplicity, the body of the tubes can be left undressed; however, if you prefer the brass tube bodies to have a silver appearance, rub them gently with fine wire wool. For a wing, use a single bunch of bucktail hair long enough to extend ¼in

(20mm) beyond the rear of the tube. Now, all there is to do is to fit a small length of silicone rubber sleeving to the rear of the tube to help keep the treble in line.

Overcoming Problems with Tubes

Some anglers do not use tube flies, but in this they are really missing out on a lure that has accounted for the downfall of countless salmon. There are many occasions throughout a season when a tube is the only realistic option, and it is foolish to forgo intentionally these highly versatile items of tackle just because you dislike them. One of the main reasons for anglers disliking tubes is that they get tired with the treble hook coming free of the sleeving and hinging around the nylon. Usually this happens because the internal diameter of the tubing used to perform this function is over-wide for the hook being used; it is quite a common problem when using needle eye trebles. One simple way of curing it is to use a sleeving with a smaller internal diameter; and if the latter is not available, then a larger hook will work equally as well. The best solution however, is to use an X1 outpoint treble from Partridge, or the Rob Wilson CS9 treble hook instead. These hooks have a larger, rounder eye than the needle-eyed versions, and as a

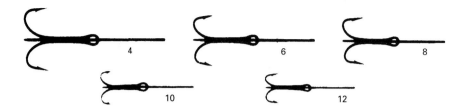

Fig 10 Partridge PM tube fly treble hooks.

result will fit much more snugly into the tubing. Alternatively if you do not have sleeving with a smaller internal diameter, or want to fit a larger hook, you can make use of the extra nylon you normally cut off after tying on the hook: instead of shortening it, this surplus can be left intact and folded back along the leader; it can then be pushed into the hole in the plastic liner at the rear of the tube.

A simple yet innovative technique of keeping the shank of the treble hook in the same plane as the body of the tube is to use the Partridge PM Tube Fly Hook code X7 designed by Peter Masting. With these hooks no sleeving is necessary as they have a spike incorporated into them which you simply push into the plastic liner of the tube (*see* Fig 10).

Modern Trends

One modern trend concerning tubes is to tie them with the hair secured to the rear instead of the front; by so doing, the movement of the hair is not restricted by the body of the tube, but can sway back and forth with the incident current much more easily. Because it can do this, the fly will

have an attractiveness which conventionally tied tubes lack. The length of wing on these tubes can be as long or as short as one likes, though a wing two to three times the length of the tube itself is the most common. Tube flies tied in this fashion usually have brass tube bodies; however, I see no reason why plastic or aluminium ones cannot be used.

Although tube flies are a firm favourite with many UK anglers, they do not seem to have caught on in North America. Perhaps the reason for this is that in many rivers it is illegal to use treble hooks. Although tubes are not as popular as they are here in the UK, a number of North American anglers are, nonetheless, starting to realize their attributes. In order to use them they employ a single or double hook with a ring eye, and a silver hook is preferred to provide flash when the current works the hair. The eyes of these hooks are sometimes forced into the rear of the tube, but the most common practice is to let the tube remain free of the hook. Provided the fly is fished in the conventional wet fly fashion – that is, down and across – the force of the water keeps the tube in contact with the hook.

5 MAKE MINE A ...

A long-running debate which frequently raises its head in the angling press is which hook – single, double or treble – provides the best hook-hold on fish. These articles subsequently always produce a flux of letters to the editors. It is certainly good for the sport that such articles do persuade anglers to put pen to paper to express their own views, but many of them in fact miss the true point of the issue: instead of

When choosing a fly, how many anglers consider the hooking quality of the hook to which it is tied?

simply asking which hook gives the better hold on fish, they should also be looking at which hook is the most likely to get a hold. Some people may think that the best 'holder' of fish must be the same as the one that grips the most fish, but this is not the case, and there is no guarantee that the hook which gives the best hold will grip more fish than any other. In this chapter I look at both of these aspects.

THE IDEAL HOOK

So, which hook should you use? Well, the answer at first may seem simple: it is the one which lands the most fish. However, each hook style has certain advantages over the others, which means that each is best served to fulfil certain tasks – so there is no 'one' hook, and the ideal hook is the one which performs the job for which it was specifically designed. Regardless of whether it has one, two or three cusps, the hooking efficiency of any hook is dependent on five things:
(1) The pulling force.
(2) The angle of pull.
(3) Barb size and position, and the distance it is placed from the point.
(4) The width of the 'gape' and the depth of the 'throat'.
(5) The way in which the fish takes hold of it.
Some anglers will be thinking the sharpness of the point must also be considered. Now, if there was a vast difference between the sharpness of hooks of all the current different makes, I would say yes, but the hooks made by all the reputable manufacturers mentioned in this book have excellent, needle-like points, and so I cannot see that it is an issue at all.

Pulling Force

Obviously it will take less force to pull a single-point hook home than it will a double or a treble of the same size with identical specifications, that is, barb size and position, wire gauge, width of gape and so on. However, single hooks have only one point with which to catch skin tissue, so there is only one source of indentation available at any one time. Further, unless the point addresses the salmon's mouth correctly, the chances are that it will not complete the task. Having said this, if it does find skin it will require much less force than an equivalent-sized double or treble to bury itself up to the bend.

Double hooks, on the other hand, have two points slanted away from each other and so will be more likely to secure a grip than their single-pointed counterparts; this angle of slant ranges from about 20 to 65 degrees depending on the size of the hook. As well as this, the distance between the points also increases: in the larger sizes, 2s and 4s, the distance between the points can be as much as ⅜in (1cm), depending on the make and style. This gap does allow them a good chance of finding skin; however, they do require more force to pull them up past the barbs. Nowadays when using double hooks I tend to use nothing larger than a size 6, as I have found from experience that the smaller sizes give a firmer hold. Perhaps this is due to the fact that in the smaller sizes both of the points generally take a grip, unlike the larger sizes when only one takes hold.

A treble hook, although it has three separate hooks, does not in fact provide 360 degrees of hooking power, as some writers would have us believe: they have three separate points positioned 120 degrees apart, and thus each of them stands a 33.33

per cent chance of securing a hold. In fact a treble hook can only provide 360 degrees of hooking potential if it is rotating, as when used with a Devon Minnow, or if all three hook points happen to come into contact with skin at the same time; and the likelihood of this occurring with a large size 2 or 4 treble is extremely unlikely. Even when a small treble is pulled into the confined corner of the 'scissors', all three points seldom penetrate skin. When fly fishing, trebles do not revolve as they do when used on a Devon Minnow trace, but remain comparatively fixed – I say 'comparatively' because if fished in a strong current they can roll from side to side; at times it is perhaps this movement which encourages fish to take, even though it is inevitably somewhat limited by the nylon.

Although the three points will remain at 120 degrees to each other, as the hook size increases, so does the distance between the hook points. At first this may seem to be a distinct advantage, as the hook will be covering a larger area and will therefore be more likely to find skin. However, since the points are more 'outlying', it means that there is a much higher chance of only one of the points taking hold, and if this happens the chances are that the hook will sway from side to side during the playing of a fish; should this occur the dimensions of the hook hole will almost certainly increase, resulting in the barb losing its grip. (This swaying is something which is not unique to trebles, it also occurs with single hooks.) For this reason I tend to use trebles only in the smaller sizes. Since the points on double hooks are placed closer together, there is a far greater chance that both will penetrate skin and so will not be able to sway.

Finally regarding 'pulling force', a number of anglers are starting to use fly lines with low-stretch cores, because they believe these lines facilitate greater energy transfer. I have no doubt that fly lines with low-stretch cores *will* transfer more energy, but I am not so sure they put any more fish on the bank.

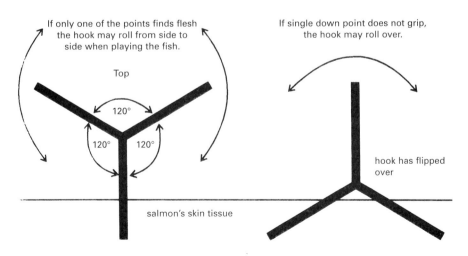

Fig 11 Hooks viewed from the front.

Single, double and treble. All will bring fish to the bank.

Angle of Pull

Generally it is the angle from which the hook is pulled into the skin which determines its hooking efficiency. On this there are two governing factors: the position of the hook in relation to the fly line being used when the angler tightens when feeling the weight of the fish; and the direction in which the fish moves after taking hold of the fly. (With reference to Fig 12 I shall look at some of the possibilities which can arise.)

When Fishing the Conventional Down-and-across Method with a Floating Line
In this instance the fly will, if fished properly, be a short distance beneath the surface (*see* Fig 13a). The distance between the two will depend on who is fishing, the angle at which the line is cast and the quality of their line control, the pace of the current, the size and weight of the hook and the amount of dressing used. Some fish will mouth our fly prior to heading and tailing on the surface, ie the fly has been

A Hook is pulled upward. This happens when hook is fished below fly line.
B Hook is pulled straight. This happens when both hook and fly line are fished at the same depth.
C Hook is pulled down. This happens when hook is fished above line.

Fig 12 Hook reaction to different angles of pull.

taken by the time the head has appeared; others will not take it until they have rolled back below the surface. Not all fish, however, will announce their presence with a visual display when coming to a fly fished with a floater – I have taken fish which have left not a mark on the surface, when my flies were barely two inches deep. Very often the first indication we get that a fish has taken hold it is a downward pull on the rod tip.

The angle at which the pulling force is applied by the angler will depend mainly on the height the rod tip is above the surface of the water when the strike of the fish is felt. If outpointed treble hooks are being used, the bottom point is the one which initially finds flesh, but the chances of this securing a good hold is remote, as this point of the hook will be starting to angle through the flesh as the rod is raised (*see* Fig 12 A1). As the rod is raised more to bring the hooks home, the eye of the hook will be lifted further and any hold which the lower hook point has contracted will be lost (*see* Fig 12 A2). At this stage we have no hold on the fish, and if it has its mouth open, it is lost. But provided it has closed its mouth before the bottom hook comes out, the two upper hooks will find a resting place in the roof of the mouth.

Sometimes the two upper hooks will find the centre of the roof, but more often than not they will be to one side.

The side to which they fasten will depend in which direction the fish turns and moves after taking. If it turns down and away from the angler, the hooks will be in its upper right jaw; whereas if it turns down and towards the angler after taking the fly, they will be in the upper left-hand jaw. This last is generally what occurs when the angler is fishing from the bank. However, if he is wading relatively deep and fishing with a low rod point, the pull on the hook is more direct and the bottom hook will find a hold in the tongue, or the lower jaw. Again, the exact location will depend on the direction the fish turns after taking. By looking at where the hooks have located themselves we can sometimes figure out the direction in which the fish turned after taking the fly.

It may be thought that the hooks will find themselves in the scissors if the fish turns: this is seldom the case with trebles, however, particularly if the salmon has closed its mouth prior to turning away. Most of the photographs of fish that you see in the angling press where the fly is shown embedded in the scissors have been specially set up, and more often than not the hooks have been removed from their original place of incision and moved to the corner of the jaws before the photograph is taken. I must confess I have been guilty of doing this myself when taking photographs for books or magazine articles.

When the Fly is Fished at the Same Depth as the Fly Line

This is shown in Fig 13b. Since the hook is fishing at the depth of the line it must be on a sinking line (unless, of course, we are fishing a dry fly). At first it might be thought that when the hooks are pulled into skin tissue they will be pulled upwards as A1 and A2 in Fig 12. This is not the case, however, and usually by the time the angler feels the fish when fishing a sinking line the hooks have already established themselves, especially if they

happen to be small, chemically sharpened doubles or outpoint trebles.

We cannot predict or guarantee the way a fish will move after it has taken our fly; however, for the purposes of explanation I shall assume in this case the fish has tailed back in the current without either turning away or heading downwards back to its lie. Usually this type of take is quite soft. When the fish initially pulls on the line, the angler, not sure whether it is a fish or not, tentatively raises his rod to find out. As he does, so the line entering the water immediately in front of the rod is lifted from the water surface. Some anglers may think that as the line lifts from the water, the fly will also be pulled upwards; however, although this may be the case with a floating line, it is not the case with a sinker, and the section of sunk line near the fly will initially remain in the same plane

The decaying remains of a Tay kelt. With all the dentition shown it is a wonder that any cock fish during the autumn come to the bank at all.

as the fly, the fly and line merely moving forward upstream.

It is during the time of the forward motion of this sunk section of line that the hook points will be pulled in, the pulling force being in the same plane in which the line is moving at the time. If the fish at this stage stops moving back in the current, the 'tightening' force exerted will be almost the same as the force used by the angler when he lifted his rod tip when feeling for the fish. I say almost, because most fly lines on the market have some inherent stretch, as does the nylon leader, so not all the energy will therefore be transmitted to the hook points. On the other hand, if the fish is tailing back in the current, any

elasticity in the line is irrelevant because the fish is moving contra to the pull applied by the angler. If the single downward-point hook of the treble in Fig 12B happens to find skin, it will usually pull itself well in around the bend, and if the salmon has closed its mouth around the fly, all three hooks can find themselves buried; moreover, since the forward pulling force is exerted directly, the hooks which do find flesh are generally buried deep, well up around the bend to the shank.

Even if fish move differently from the ways described – that is, away or towards the angler – provided the fly is fishing at the same depth as the line at the moment of the take, the fish will as a rule be well

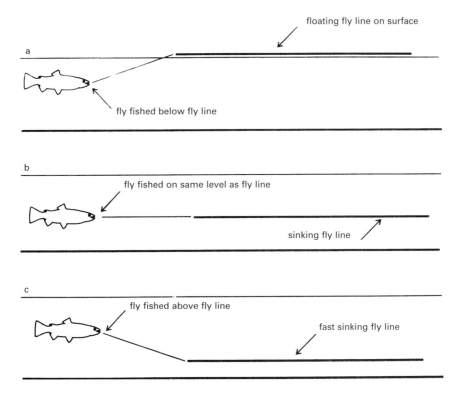

Fig 13 Status of fly in relation to fly line.

Executing a double Spey cast with a single-handed rod on the Swallow Braes Beat of the River Doon.

hooked. Again this is due to the initial lateral pull of the line as the angler raises his rod tip on feeling the fish.

When the Fly is Fished above the Fly Line
This is shown in Fig 13c, and usually occurs when a lightweight buoyant fly is fished with a sinking line. On feeling the fish take, the angler lifts the rod tip and as he does so the fly is pulled downwards: as a result the fish is generally hooked somewhere in the lower jaw, the exact location depending which way the fish turns after taking. If it tails back in the current without turning, it will more than likely be hooked in the tongue. It might be thought that if its mouth is open at this stage the hooks will be pulled out, but this is not the case, and

the lower single hook will assume a position to that shown in Fig 12C.

There is no guarantee that fish will come to our flies in the fashions described: salmon are quite individual and can come to our flies in a variety of ways. I recall a fish my wife hooked when fishing in the fashion shown in Fig 13c in the Market Pool on the Mochrum Park beat of the River Bladnoch a few miles below Kirkowan during the October of 1995. The fish was hooked on the lower left jaw, with both the points of the double hook holding just forward of the scissors. So what's so strange about this occurrence? Well, had my wife been fishing from the right-hand bank, this would have been the most likely place to have found the hooks. As it happened, however, she was fishing from the

Mary unhooking the fish described. The fly can quite easily be seen in the corner of the lower left jaw.

left bank. Talking about the capture of her fish later that evening, it transpired she was casting square across the pool and had just started to strip in line when the fish took. When she felt the gentle pull on the line she uncertainly lifted her rod tip to ascertain if yet another leaf had attached itself to the hook, at which point the line was pulled quickly downstream, away from her and then quickly upstream.

What I think happened is this: on seeing the fly shoot past it, the fish turned quickly out of its lie which was tight against the far bank, into the mainstream side of the pool. It then swung round in the current, away from her, and proceeded to move back upstream to its lie. I am sure it did not actually mouth the fly until it was facing downstream, and had we viewed this

'take' from above I suspect we would have seen the fish complete a full 360-degree clockwise turn. The fish incidentally was a cock salmon weighing 7lb and covered in sea-lice.

Other Occurrences

The hooks do not all end up in the lower jaw as in the incident just described, but often find other locations. There is the fish which comes to a lightweight fly presented with a sinking line in a stream with a strong flow: in this instance it will not have a chance to move far before the current brings the hook points into play. If we suspect a fish has taken our fly and raise our rods to find out, the fly, if it has not been taken, will simply move forward in the current. As soon as its forward motion is impeded, however, as when a fish takes hold, the only way the eye of the hook can initially travel is down. When this happens the lower hook points will find a hold in the lower jaw, and how far they are pulled in will correspond to the distance the eye of the hook travels downward before it comes up against tissue. At this instant, hook-point penetration stops, and as a result it is impossible for the points of the hook to penetrate deep. Sometimes they will go in far enough for the barbs to grip, but if they don't they will only achieve a transitory hold. As the rod is raised further the fish feels the pressure, turns down and makes back to its lie, and as this occurs the eye of the hook will be pulled in an upward direction resulting in the lower hook points gouging themselves *out* of this initial hold. When this happens when

we are using a treble hook, the two upper hooks often find themselves pulled into the upper jaw. This relocation of the hook is due to the salmon taking the fly down below the level of the fly line.

If this sort of take occurs when fishing with a double or single hook it is unlikely we would get a second hold on the fish; all we would experience is a tentative pluck followed by a 'dead' line. In my experience a lightweight fly for this type of fishing is a much better hooker if it employs a treble, because we then stand a far better chance of gaining a fatal hold. As with the double hook we get a draw on the line, but instead of going 'dead', a hefty pull shortly after this tells us the fish is secured. This happens when the fish kicks down, bending the rod: as we feel the fish kick, the two upper hooks at this time are establishing themselves in the roof of the mouth.

Fishing the quiet, but often difficult water between two channels.

There is no doubt in my mind that a fly dancing above a fly line is a good way of attracting fish; nevertheless, I have found that most of the fish I entice to a fly fished like this quickly throw the hook. This perhaps is my fault, because on feeling the weight of a fish I like to lift against it. Those anglers who prefer to feed slack, or who fish with a high rod point, may not experience the poor hooking I experience when the fly is 'ballooning' above a fast sinking line.

Barb Size and Position and its Distance from the Point

What is a barb? A barb is quite simply a reverse-facing spike, the function of which is to stop the hook from sliding out once it has penetrated skin tissue or bone.

Barb Size

The size of the barb on a hook is very important. For ease of incision a small, thinly cut barb inclined at a shallow angle is best; however, the hold such a barb gives is cursory. For maximum hold the barb should be 'thick' in nature with the rearmost edge positioned almost at right-angles to the point – although, needless to say, this type of barb would impede penetration. A large barb provides better holding, but in order to produce this a deeper cut must be made into the wire. A thicker-gauge wire could be used, but a hook made from such wire would require significantly greater force to make it penetrate the skin. The perfect barb should not impede penetration, yet at the same time it should stop the hook from coming out. Like every other engineering solution, the end result is one of compromise; although as far as I am concerned, most of the modern salmon fly hooks currently produced have an over-small barb.

Barb Position

All but one of the hooks currently available to salmon anglers have their barbs placed 'conventionally' on the inside of the gape. However, two ranges of hooks manufactured by Partridge and designed by Hugh Falkus have the barbs placed on the outside of the gape (*see* Fig 14), in an attempt to provide a more secure grip on fish. It was also to try and alleviate skin damage in the area bearing the pulling force, ie any pressure applied being to undamaged skin. From what I understood after reading the advertising these outbarb hooks received in the angling press, they were designed so as to allow anglers to land more fish (in that their design made them less likely to come out).

X2B Outpoint

Hugh Falkus Holdfast Outbarb

Fig 14 Hook profiles (not actual size).

Always the sceptic, I decided to do some experiments with these hooks myself. I found that they did indeed have increased gripping potential; however, it was not universal, and depended essentially on which jaw the fish was hooked in. Thus, if fish are hooked in the lower jaw, they will give a superior grip to that provided by a conventional hook: this is because the pulling force exerted by the angler comes mainly from above the fish, and so the unbarbed inner edge of the hook will be pulled into undamaged skin tissue. On the other hand, I found if fish are hooked in the upper jaw, these outbarb hooks are comparably less effective because the 'outbarbs' in this situation will be facing upwards: since the force pulling comes from *above* the fish, the angler will be pulling the hook into skin which has been damaged by the incision of the outbarb. Thus from my tests I believe that a conventionally barbed hook will provide better grip on a fish hooked in the upper jaw.

Influence of the Reel Type
Of course, having cited my findings, I am bound to say they are only relevant if a constant pressure is exerted throughout the fight, and as long as the fish behaves itself. The amount of pressure applied during the playing of a fish can vary enormously, from a steady increase applied by the angler clamping the line against the handle of the rod and pulling harder, or a succession of violent rapid changes brought about by the fish shaking its head. Many reels on the market have a pawl-and-detent drag system. If the drag is set on the heavy side, the sudden abrupt changing of the tension by the to'ing and fro'ing of the pawl in and out of the 'cog' will produce a hammer drill-type action as the back-and-forth action of the hook opens up skin tissue. Reels with disc drags like the System Twos distributed by Leeda do not do this, which is why many anglers are starting to favour them. These are only some examples, but any irregular increasing and decreasing of pressure will almost certainly increase the size of the hole made by the hook.

Being the owner of both reel types, I have found from experience that the ones which use a ratchet-type drag system are inclined to keep the fish moving more than the disc drag variety, perhaps because the ratchet vibration transmitted down the line annoys the fish more; and because the fish I take on my ratchet reels put up a more vigorous fight, they are often brought to the bank more quickly. Even so, I still enjoy fishing with disc drags, finding them more pleasant and less 'clangorous' to fish with. Regardless of the type of drag system employed in a reel, if the pressure on a fish is maintained the hook will remain firm; however, as is most often the case, when the pressure is reduced the hook will not fit so snugly and this could result in a lost fish.

Of the examples I have given, the shaking of the fish's head is the most problematic, as this action causes severe tearing of the flesh. And I can assure you, when the size of the hole increases, it matters little whether we are using an outbarb or a conventional-style hook, because either one will lose any advantage they may have had.

The Distance the Barb is Placed from the Point
This is one of the major factors determining the holding efficiency of a hook. A

In times of low water our fly will inevitably pick up weed. If it does,
remove it. I have yet to experience a salmon taking a fly with
vegetation attached.

barb which is placed any distance from the point will require the hook to penetrate further before it can come into play. On the other hand, hooks which have the barbs placed close to the point will bring the barb into employment sooner, but the hold they take up is usually in the softer outer skin tissue and it is seldom very good. Most manufacturers therefore design their hooks so that the rear-most edge of the barb is placed approximately halfway between the point and the inner edge of the bend, ie about 50 per cent of the way into the throat of the hook.

Width of the Gape and Throat

The width of the gape determines how far the point can penetrate: the larger the gape, the greater the depth of penetration.

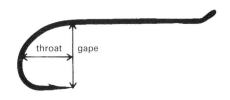

Fig 15 Width of gape and throat.

In my opinion some salmon hooks on the market have too small a gape, and as a result any pulling force applied while playing a fish will tend to tear the hooks through the thin layer of flesh. Hooks with larger gapes are more prone to penetrate bone and are therefore not so easily extracted. Although the gape determines how deep the hook can penetrate, the throat of the hook is the part which takes the force of the angler pulling, and the deeper it is the better the force is distributed, so the skin or bone tissue will be less inclined to tear. Hooks with small throats seldom provide a secure hold on fish.

The Way in which Fish Take Hold

The way a fish takes hold of our fly will determine whether or not it stays attached. If it lacks conviction, the chances are that the hooks will fail to take a secure grip regardless of which type they are. Also the direction in which a fish turns after taking hold of the fly plays a major part in determining whether or not the hooks will secure a hold. Salmon which turn towards the bank from which the angler is fishing are seldom hooked properly, while those which turn away in a wide purposeful arc are nearly always well hooked. In order to try and secure the best hook-hold, we would have to know the way in which a fish is going to react to our fly; and since fish can come to our fly in a variety of ways we cannot exercise any *one* particular method to ensure secure hooking. Fish will therefore continue to be hooked and lost, regardless of which type of hook our fly is tied on.

There has been a great deal written about how to hook salmon on the fly: some of the methods described will work some of the

time, but none will work all of the time. From experience I would suggest you do *not* adopt an all-methods approach because this only breeds uncertainty; it is far better to take up one method and stick to it.

HOOK TYPES

Each type of hook enjoys its following of loyal devotees, every one of whom will argue fervently in favour of their choice. From my own observations and conversations with many anglers and ghillies, I would say that the majority of today's anglers show a marked preference for doubles or trebles. There are still some, however, who refuse to express a liking for anything other than a single, although they do seem to be a dying breed. During my forays around Scotland in the last few years I have come across only the occasional angler using flies dressed on single hooks. One interesting thing I have noted, though, is that many of those anglers who use double or treble hooks when after salmon, will opt for a single when fishing for sea-trout. Why do they have faith in these hooks when after sea-trout, yet reject them when fishing for salmon? This has always been a mystery to me.

Regardless of which type you choose, hooks are without doubt the most important link in the chain. The mechanical stresses on a hook while playing fish are many, so it is crucial that it is capable of performing the task for which it is made. Some manufacturers make their hooks from too soft a wire, and these will bend and twist and inevitably break. Other makes I have tried have been over tempered and brittle and have ended up failing – even hooks from reputable manufacturers can fail. One

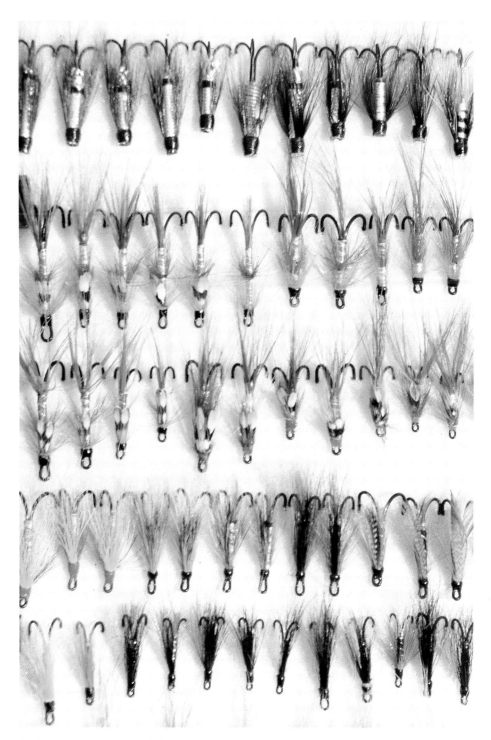

A selection of summer flies, including Keachie's Krill (second row from the top).

Let's see if this one will do the business. A large yellow fly like the one I am holding will often tempt spring fish.

Trying to stop a fish from running out of the Mill Pool on the River Doon. Four others were taken from the same pool within the space of two hours, three fish coming from the same lie.

Spey casting on the Tay.

July on the Tay. When fishing such rivers, always use a wading staff and buoyancy aid.

Knowing the water. The ghillie points out the lies.

Jock Woods netting a fish from Swallow Braes.

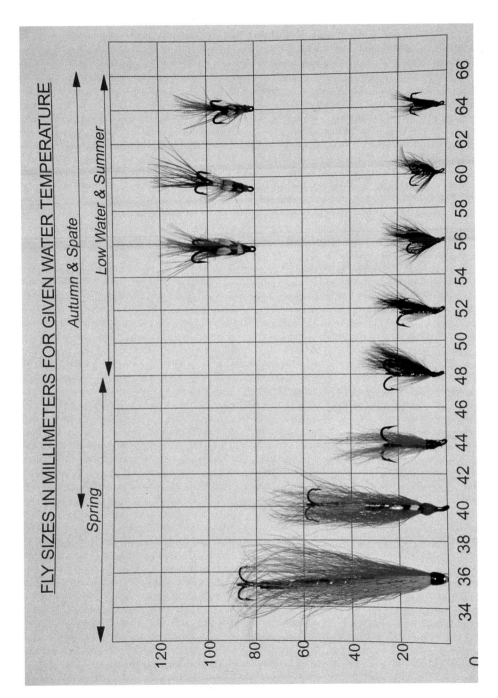

Fly sizes and colours preferred for different water heights and temperatures.

Faced with a long walk on the 'mighty' Tay.

Mary putting out a good line on the Spey at Aberlour.

The reward for persevering. A late October fish, silver-fresh and covered in sea-lice.

A fish moves in the Artist's Pool on the Findhorn.

Into an autumn fish from the Bladnoch.

Almost there.

Last light, last cast? Not likely! It often pays to fish into the darkness.

fish – a good one, as it happened – which I hooked on a treble had chewed it into an unrecognizable shape, a hook from a reputable company with world-wide recognition, not one from a cheap, bulk-lot purchase; a few seconds longer spent playing it and I would almost certainly have been deprived of my hard-earned prize.

I can also remember losing a large fish which took an Ally's Shrimp tied on a Waddington right in the tail of the Kiln Pool on the Smithston beat of the River Doon, when fishing during a summer spate. Immediately below the pool there is over 150 yards of fast, rough water, and if a fish leaves the pool you really don't stand any chance of following it. Needless to say, this fish decided to make a bolt for the tail of the pool, and I had no choice but to hold it firm. After a few minutes of applying what I can only describe as severe pressure in order to try and stop it entering the maelstrom below, it abandoned its quest and ran up into the quieter water in the centre of the pool – and as it did so, we parted company. At first I thought that perhaps the hooks had torn themselves out; on inspection, however, I discovered that one of the points on the treble had sheared at the bend. It was later suggested that perhaps I had inadvertently knocked the fly off a rock during a back cast and weakened it; I don't think so.

The Manufacture of Modern Hand-made Hooks

A hook begins life as a length of high-carbon steel wire: this is straightened and cut to the appropriate length, and both ends

Fish which come to the surface early in the fight are often lightly hooked. In this case the hooks held fast.

are then pointed (singles and doubles only). Next the barb is fashioned by making a small cut at the back of the point (though take care not to make it too deep); normally it does not exceed 20 per cent of the wire diameter.

The bend is then fashioned by taking the wire round an appropriate former, and it is cold forged to strengthen to the heel of the bend. Bowing is the next process, where the wire is taken round a small stud to form the eye; this is then bent up or down depending on the style required.

Once the hooks have been formed and bent to shape, they are hardened and tempered in a controlled atmosphere. Some ranges will then have their points sharpened: the chemical used attacks the thinnest area of the wire, ie the point, as a result of which process any rough edges are eaten away to produce a finer point. The length of time the hooks are left in contact with the chemical is crucial: too long, and the point will be dulled and weakened.

After sharpening they are chemically cleaned, then bronzed or blackened. Some manufacturers, such as Partridge, have ranges of hooks with a special Niflor finish, a nickel/phosphorous protective coating which incorporates PTFE; as a result the surface of the hook is very hard and slippery. Partridge claim their Niflor hooks have a low friction coefficient so the points penetrate more easily.

The Structure of the Salmon's Mouth

The salmon's mouth, its dentition, the firmness of its skin tissue and the way in which it seizes its prey, are all issues worthy of discussion, considering the prime function of the hook is to secure a hold

within it. This mouth has evolved through many generations to catch and secure prey, so if a salmon takes hold of something with conviction there is little chance of it escaping. Like other piscean predators that feed on other fish, if a salmon catches a large prey fish which it cannot fit entirely into its mouth when this is closed, it targets the head; this is so that it can swallow it head first, thus ensuring that its scales and fins are positioned so they cannot stick in its throat when swallowed. When taking small prey which it can swallow with no difficulty, it simply sucks it in and closes its mouth around it, after this, like most other animals, it will press it against the roof of its mouth with its tongue in order to swallow it.

Even though salmon do not feed in freshwater, I am certain that when they attack angler's flies in the river they do so in the same way that they attack prey at sea. It used to be thought that a fly with a long trailing wing would be a poor hooker of fish; however, this idea has subsequently been proved wrong, with the Collie Dog. If the tube used with these flies is kept on the short side, the hooks frequently find themselves in the tongue or the back of the throat. However, if the tube length is overlong – that is, longer than the width of the salmon's mouth – I have found that the hooks frequently embed themselves in the *outside* of the jaw. Some anglers may consider that a fish hooked in such a place is foul-hooked: I do not. Provided the salmon has mouthed my fly properly and is clean run and not a kelt or a gravid autumn fish which I am intending to return, I have no qualms about delivering the last rites with my priest and keeping it. (However, I do not intend to embark upon a long literary argument about this.

When everything goes well.

And if a fish takes such a fly and turns with it, it is almost without exception hooked in the scissors.

The mouth of a fresh-run salmon straight in off the tide is apt to be soft, and because of this a good percentage of these fish inevitably escape the priest. When I have hooked and lost a fresh-run fish, on checking my hooks before I begin fishing again, I have frequently found skin tissue still attached to them. On entering the river, salmon grow a new set of teeth and at this time their mouth tissue remains soft: however, as the season advances the teeth start to grow longer and become attached to the bone, and the surrounding skin hardens. Since the salmon does not feed in the river I believe these teeth are for the purpose of contending with other fish in order to

secure a mate; indeed, a cock salmon with full breeding dentition is a fearsome sight. With these autumn fish, if a hook penetrates beyond the barb into the bone beneath the hardened skin it is seldom thrown. This is perhaps why fewer coloured fish during the backend come off, as compared to the softer-skinned springers and grilse that run earlier in the year.

Note that a cock fish when sexually mature develops a fleshy appendix at the front of its lower jaw called a 'kype': fish hooked here are seldom landed. If, on the other hand, the hook finds its way into the cavity in the upper jaw where the kype fits, these salmon *are* frequently landed. (I am not talking about the neb of the nose, which is a most unwished-for place to hook a fish.)

SINGLE HOOKS

For the anglers who prefer single hooks there is a bewildering assortment of styles to choose from. Partridge alone currently manufacture eleven different styles suitable for tying flies; Mustad and Kamasan also manufacture their own styles. The code M hooks made by Partridge are traditional single irons which come in sizes ranging from 5/0 down to 10 and come with a looped-up eye; these are heavyweight hooks best suited to faster runs, or when the water is carrying some extra height and colour. For medium-water heights, Partridge do a low-water version of this hook. These are code N hooks, and are made with a narrower-gauge wire, they have a longer shank with a looped-up eye and come in sizes ranging from 8/0 to 10.

Another popular style for summer fishing is the O1 Single Wilson hook, lightweight wire hooks made from a thinner-gauge wire than the code N hooks. Originally designed for top-of-the-water, dry fly fishing, they come in sizes ranging from 2 to 16. Of the three types mentioned, I would consider that these are the most popular. Having said this, some devotees of single hooks do not like them: this dislike is based on the belief that the narrower-gauge wire, while allowing easier penetration than the other two types, is more inclined to pull out because it gashes skin tissue.

One other single that is gaining popularity with the single hook brigade is the Cs10/1 Bartleet Traditional Fly Hooks for tying shrimp patterns. Having a curved shank they are ideally shaped to represent shrimp flies. Sizes range from 3/0 to 10.

During the autumn when there is an abundance of leaves in the water, many anglers opt for a fly tied on a single hook. The reason for this is that these hooks are much less prone to impaling themselves into leaves, something which double and treble hooks do with annoying regularity; there is nothing more frustrating than constantly having to hand line in twenty or more yards of line to clear the hooks of sodden decaying foliage.

Probably the most famous angler to use single hooks was A.H.E. Wood. He preferred to use long-shank light summer hooks, because he believed they hooked and held fish better. In correspondence to other eminent anglers of the time, Wood wrote that he used these hooks because he thought that the fish took less notice of them, and that they allowed one to have a small fly tied on a longer hook. Arthur Wood did not like small hooks, as he believed small hooks dressed full length did not provide the same hold on fish that a partially-dressed, long-shanked hook gave. He also wrote that these long-shank flies gave a better 'grip' on the fish, particularly if they were fresh run. How things have changed, because the style of fly that he developed is now passed over by many of today's anglers, the majority preferring a more mobile hairwing pattern tied on either a small, low-water double or a treble. Perhaps he had a point, however, regarding the hooking of fresh-run fish.

The reason Wood favoured the long-shank single hook with the dressing on the front third was because he firmly believed that a fly dressed in this style on this type of hook would hook more fish well back in the mouth; although he in fact only hooked about 50 per cent of the total number of fish that he rose. For instance in April and May, while fishing at Cairnton, he hooked 336, killing only 179 of them, i.e. 53 per cent. One possible reason for this is because Wood favoured feeding slack line to a taking fish, a method that does not favour a largish hook with a wide gape, such as Wood used. During communication with Barry, Wood wrote about his anxiety and failure when it came to hooking and losing fish. Both Barry and Crossley had far better success rates by fishing with doubles and by lifting against the pull of taking fish, and by doing this, killed a significantly higher proportion of fish which came to their flies than Wood did. Having said this, during the time that he leased the fishing at Cairnton, Wood landed no fewer than 3,490 salmon. Incidentally, when Barry fished at Careysville Cairnton and Tulchan with single hooks during March, April and May of the same year he hooked 323 fish, killing 176, that is, just a little over 54 per cent of the total number hooked. Looking at the statistics given for both anglers' catches, it can be seen that there was only 1 per cent difference in their hooking-to-landing ratio, even though each used his own, different method of hooking fish. It was after this incident that Barry started to favour double hooks.

On hooking fish, Wood became engrossed in correspondence concerning presenting the fly at the right angle in order for the fish to take it properly. He wanted fish to take the fly 'broadside on', and described his technique further by saying that he tried either to keep a long straight line when the fly was swimming at right-angles down and across, or by manoeuvring his line, tried to keep the last 3 or 4 yards of fly line near his leader slack. He used this approach so that the fish could take a few feet of line before he felt the pull on it, and stated at length that by using

these two techniques of hooking fish he never had any pulls or plucks. This I must say I find hard to believe, although he did say that he had a few 'misses', making his tale more plausible. The reason he gave for these was that sometimes a fly could pass through a fish's mouth without it taking hold, especially if the fly were lying flat on the salmon's tongue.

In this he was absolutely correct, and I find myself in complete agreement. There are occasions when salmon will demonstrate the annoying behaviour of taking a fly, but remaining open-mouthed. Regardless of whether we are fishing a single, double, or treble hook these fish are the very devil to hook. If you observe this type of taking behaviour, feeding slack line will sometimes bring about a hooked fish, because the current pulling on the line brings the fly into the corner of the salmon's jaws. Very often, though, the clarity of the water does not make it possible to employ such a tactic. These fish will swing round in the current unseen while holding the fly in a pocket of water within their mouths. I have seen fish swim with a fly in this fashion the full traverse of a pool, the angler remaining unaware that anything was happening. When this kind of take occurs it often feels as though the current has lost its pull on the fly and most anglers put it down to the nuances of the current within the flow.

When a fish takes hold of a fly properly, the first thing it generally does after closing its jaws is press it against the roof of its mouth; this brings the fly into contact with a number of taste receptors and gives the salmon information which will help it to investigate what it has taken hold of. When it does this, one of two things can occur: first, if the hook shank and point are parallel and true to the tongue, with the bend of the hook at right-angles, the upward compressing force exerted by the fish will bring the point of the hook into contact with the tongue. If this occurs, any turning away by the fish, or tightening of the line by the angler, or the current pulling at it, will provide further point penetration. On the other hand, if the hook shank and point of the hook are not true – that is, if they are off balance – it will lie down on its side when pushed against the roof of the salmon's mouth. If the hook lies flat the angler still stands a chance of hooking the fish, especially if it turns away; but it also goes without saying that the salmon may equally as well eject it, because tissue penetration has not taken place.

In order to prove this point to any sceptics, I suggest they take a single hook and place it between forefinger and thumb. Place it so that the rear of the shank is running along the underside of your forefinger and the point is lying parallel to the underside of your thumb. Gently press both fingers together: if the hook is standing true at this point it will still be in an upright position. Now take hold of the eye of the hook and pull slowly forwards: *be careful*, as the point of the hook will now start to penetrate skin. On the other hand, if the hook was not standing straight it will now be lying down on its side between your two fingers and would come free if pulled: this is because its point is much thinner in diameter than the shank and so there is vacant space around it. In fact, in order for the point to penetrate flesh it must be offset from the shank. Some anglers who prefer fishing with single hooks know this, and modify their hooks accordingly by twisting the bend of the hook out of alignment with the shank. Even though hook

makers appreciate that a hook with an offset point provides superior hooking, no manufacturer as far as I am aware produces single irons with suchlike points, onto which flies can be dressed. Hooks with an offset point will screw their way into flesh which standard hooks at best may only scratch. Anglers who fish the worm know from experience that a hook with an offset point gives far superior hooking to one which has the point in line. Mustad's 80500 'Professional' single hooks have their points slanted down and away from the plane of the shank. Provided the hook stays upright, any force pulling it forward will also drive the point downwards when it contacts flesh.

Another well known advocate of the single hook was the late Reg Righyni, especially when he was fishing with the floating line. The reason for this was that he liked to present thinly dressed flies below the surface at the 'correct' depth, and he also liked to hold the rod point relatively high, between 45 and 60 degrees to the surface of the water. By holding his rod thus, droop was created in the line between the rod tip and the water, and this meant that fish rising to his fly would be able to take it and move away without encountering any immediate resistance. He practised this method of hooking because he believed that a time lag was imperative between the salmon taking the fly and the angler bending the rod against the weight of the fish to set the hooks – he believed that when this method of hooking was employed, single hooks would invariably find the maxillary bone at the corner of the mouth. He disliked double and treble hooks because he felt that the only place they could secure a good hold was the inside corner of the jaw. In this I do not

Mary playing a fish on the Bladnoch.

The same fish almost ready for beaching.

agree. His belief was based on the concept that the additional points these hooks have would unavoidably find the softer, 'less desirable' skin tissue forward of the jaw bone. I cannot dispute the fact that the corner of the mouth, ie the maxillary bone, provides considerable holding on a hook, but it is not the only place in a salmon's mouth where a two- or three-pointed hook can secure a hold sure enough to land fish.

DOUBLE HOOKS

Double hooks come in as many varieties as singles; Partridge, for instance, currently produce eight styles which are favoured by salmon anglers. Code P are the heavyweight double versions of the code M singles, and are most suitable when we need to present a fly a little deeper than we would for conventional floating line presentation, especially if the water has not quite warmed sufficiently during the late spring months. Needless to say, these hooks are heavier, size for size, than their single counterparts and so flies with identical dressings will tend to fish deeper in the water. The sizes range from 2 to 12.

Somewhere I once read that 'salmon show no interest in mid-water flies': what rubbish! During the difficult changeover days which occur around the spring and autumn equinoxes, a mid-water fly is often the only method that will tempt fish. The code Q1 hooks are ideal for this type of fishing: these have an upturned eye and come with a long shank, and are widely used for floating line work during late spring and summer once the water has warmed; being lighter than the code P doubles they will pattern for pattern fish higher in the water.

These hooks come in sizes 3/0 to 12. Partridge Wilson low-water doubles, code Q2, are lightweight hooks. Size for size they have a longer shank than the code P and Q1s and are very popular for low-water summer fishing when a sparsely dressed, nebulous type fly, fished high in the water is desired. These low-water hooks are now also manufactured with a Niflor finish, code GRSQ2.

The R1A doubles are bronze-finished, down-eyed hooks with a Limerick bend and come in sizes 2 to 12. They are generally applied as trout hooks, but should not be dismissed by salmon anglers – many discerning salmon anglers I know put them to good advantage. Having a down eye they can be used in faster, streamier flows where the conventional up-eyed hooks may skate; Norwegian anglers have been using down-eyed hooks to advantage in their fast-running rivers for many years.

A relatively new hook is the R3HF outbarb double invented by Hugh Falkus. These come in sizes 6 to 14, and are relatively short in the shank with a straight eye. The most noticeable difference to other hooks is that the barb is on the outside (the outbarb hooking characteristics of the Hugh Falkus range of hooks are discussed earlier in the chapter).

The Advantages of Using Double Hooks

There are some anglers who do not like double hooks because they believe the additional bend will act as a lever and pry the other out, if only one of the points takes hold. Perhaps on occasions when using the longer-shank, low-water doubles this can happen, but with the shorter-shank hooks I think it highly unlikely; I do not believe

Mary Keachie playing a Doon fish. Five times down the pool, five fish.

that double hooks 'fall out' with the frequency that some writers infer. One significant advantage of a double hook is that it cannot lie flat in the way that a single hook tends to do; and with their double keels these hooks seldom swim askew. However, since a salmon's tongue does not have a flat surface, one 'keel' will inevitably come into contact with it before the other, and as a result of this irregularity the hook is often knocked off balance; in other words, when pressed by the tongue against the roof of the mouth it will not lie down flat, but will flip over instead. When this occurs, one of the points may penetrate the tongue, or the softer flesh between the tongue and the inner ridge of the upper or lower jaw bones, particularly if in the same instant the fish turns away with it, or the angler tightens on feeling the fish. More often than not, though, the hook will flip over, and if 'pulled home' at this time the points will, without exception, connect with and enter the hard flesh in the roof of the salmon's mouth. Frequently when I have hooked a salmon on a fly tied on a double hook I find it upside down with the points

well embedded in the roof of its mouth, and as far as I am concerned this can only happen in two possible ways, as I have explained above, or because my fly was fishing upside down when the fish took hold of it. Now, this may be the order with some anglers, but it is not the case with mine – my flies do not fish upside down!

In my opinion the 'off-balance' characteristic alone would argue a strong case for double hooks over singles; but it is very difficult to change the minds of those who are set in their ways of thinking, especially those of salmon fishermen, and particularly if their methods of fishing have brought them past success.

TREBLE HOOKS

At the present time Partridge manufacture five treble hooks designed specifically for dressing flies on, and another five which are suitable for use with Waddingtons or tubes. They also produce a treble hook with outbarbs designed by Hugh Falkus, code GRS X8, for tying hairwing salmon flies or for use with tubes. All of the treble hooks they make are outpoints. The first outpoint hooks were manufactured by Martins of Scotland.

Partridge code X treble hooks have at least a 5 degree outpoint, meaning that the point is out of line with the shank of the hook by 5 degrees. Many anglers prefer outpoint hooks because of their superior hooking qualities; hooks with the points in line with the shank tend merely to scratch any skin tissue they come into contact with, particularly if they are pulled directly. A non-outpoint hook will only penetrate deeply if the shank is veered away from the horizontal plane; in other words, if the necessary angle is produced so that a point can take hold. Outpoint trebles provide positive penetration of the skin when pulled against tissue, even when the shank remains true; thus any forward pulling force will drive the points down as soon as they meet with any resistance, something which cannot happen with hooks that have their points in line with their shanks.

The X2B hooks made by Partridge are a long-shank treble with an up eye. These come in sizes ranging from 2 to 16, and are a firm favourite with many anglers; they are very similar in appearance to the Esmond Drury treble. A number of anglers prefer the Drury treble to the X2B because they believe it provides superior hooking. Whether this is true or not, I don't know. I use both types regularly throughout the season and I must say that up to now I haven't noticed any difference in hooking command between the two. The Drury trebles were first patented and introduced in 1964; up to this time most fly fishers made do with singles and doubles, and treble hooks were used mainly by the spinning fraternity. Knowing the advantages that a treble has over a single or double hook, Richard Waddington in his book *Salmon Fishing, A New Philosophy* advocated the use of a small treble for fly fishing; he shows one attached to the 'Rational' fly. The rest, as they say, is history.

For those who like a fly tied on an extra-long shank hook, Partridge provide the CS12 and the CS18: the CS12 is similar to the X2B treble, and the CS18, originally designed for sea-trout, is fast becoming popular with anglers who do not like to use Waddington shanks. The CS12s come in sizes ranging from 2 to 12, while the CS18 hooks come in only three sizes: 12 (35mm), 14 (30mm) and 16 (26mm).

Partridge outpoint treble hook codes X1 Sl, X3 Sl, and also the Rob Wilson XX CS Sl outpoint treble, come with a silver finish. Some anglers like to use these to add a touch of flash to their Waddingtons or tubes; certainly Waddingtons and tubes which have a silver treble attached have an attractiveness in the water which they lack when adorned with a black hook, and recently I have noticed that some anglers are now using the smaller sizes of these silver hooks on which to tie up Silver Stoat's Tails. No body material is used, they simply lash a few strands of stoat's tail hair, or black squirrel hair behind the eyes of the hooks. Other anglers use these silver hooks because they think they will not be so conspicuous as black ones; they believe the silvered hooks will become 'invisible' to the fish by reflecting the colours around them. This thinking is without doubt progressive; however, I only see 'invisible' hooks being of advantage if a fish has been hooked before. If it hasn't I don't think it will associate any danger with a hook, and because of this I see no positive advantage by trying to hide it. As a rule the first fly a fish takes is its last.

6 ADVANCED SPEY CASTING

This chapter is not intended for those who wish to learn how to Spey cast, it is for the angler who has learned the basics and wants to progress beyond the realms of 'average'. Nevertheless, even if you have not learned to Spey cast, it will hopefully aid your understanding of this most useful method of casting.

ASSEMBLING A ROD CORRECTLY

Before even attempting to Spey cast the joints of the rod must be assembled and secured correctly. The standard practice among many anglers is simply to push the male and female joints together until they feel tight. However, although spigots are tapered to fit inside the female ferrule and may *feel* tight when pushed together, these joints are bound to work loose when the rod is twisting and turning during a Spey cast. Thus the push-together-assembly technique may suffice for the overhead cast, but it is totally inadequate for Spey casting. In order to assemble a rod correctly for Spey casting the joints should be pushed and twisted together. Initially the rod rings between any two sections should be about 30 degrees out of alignment when the rod ferrules and spigots are pushed together; then as the two joints become tight-fitting, the assembly procedure should be finished by twisting the female joint with a downward pushing action over the spigot in order to bring the rod rings into alignment.

Taping the Joints

Once the joints are 'screwed' together, the next thing is to secure them with tape. Many anglers use masking tape for this, but personally I don't like this type because once it gets wet – which it will, let me assure you, even on a dry day – it will come undone due to the glue losing its adhesive qualities. My own preference is to use either electrical PVC tape or amalgamating tape as used by telephone engineers; these should be stretched and wound in the same direction as the female joint was twisted down over the male spigot and the joints will then be perfectly secure. I have an 'interesting' anecdote concerning taping: on one of my courses I was showing students how to assemble a rod correctly and discovered I had left my own spool of tape in the back of my car. On inquiring if anyone had by chance brought along some tape, the ghillie in attendance to my party retorted 'I never tape up the joints on my rods'. I queried his approach, and his response was, 'By not taping up the joints I can see them

Advanced Spey casting starts even before we wet a line. Here I am taping the joints to prevent breakage.

Subsequent to taping the joints it is advisable to check the rod ring alignment. If the rod rings are out of alignment our line will not be cast so nicely.

Placing the reel on the rod. This task is best left until the joints have been taped.

Threading the fly line through the rod rings. It is well worth checking that the line is put through all the rings. If one is overlooked, the fly line will not shoot properly.

working loose and give them a tighten'! I was astounded by his reply, because not only was he a man with many years experience, he was also a 'qualified' game angling instructor who had been examined by 'the' leading body. (As it happened, somebody had brought along tape and I proceeded with my lesson, much to his annoyance.)

Overfit Joints

Many rod manufacturers are now starting to produce their rods with overfit joints, though these must still be taped in order to stop the two sections working loose. Since there is a decided 'step down' between the sections of these rods the joins can become rather bulky in appearance, especially when using a tape which is narrow in width.

To Spey cast without first taping up the joints is asking for an expensive repair. This angler would suffer no such expense.

When tape of a narrow gauge – ½in (12mm) or less – is used, quite a number of closely overlapping turns must be placed around the rim of the female section before the tape can be wound down and around the male section of the rod. In some instances when the number of turns has been excessive I have seen fly lines rub along the tape, and when this occurs our casting distance will be reduced. One way of producing a nice thin joint with overfit rods is to use tape of ¾in (19mm) or more; then we can take the tape down around the rim of the female section before continuing it on down over the male section.

It has always surprised me why some manufacturer has not come up with a rod joint which does not need to be taped. All that is needed are a spigot and ferrule which are not circular in shape: tapered oval or square would be much better. In this day and age I would have thought that joints shaped thus would not deliver too much of an engineering problem to manufacturers.

ADOPTING A COMFORTABLE HOLD

Now we must learn to adopt a hold on the rod which will be comfortable, while at the same time allowing us the necessary leverage to lift, cast and control line. Some instructors will tell you to place your right hand as near to the top of the handle as possible. However, many rods on the market have an over-long handle, which means that if the person is small, he or she will need to adopt a hunched position over the rod. Also, in order to achieve this 'much postulated' position, the arm usually has to be extended fully and as a result the elbow soon becomes tired from taking the strain. Even though carbon rods are extremely light, they will cause discomfort if held thus for anything other than the shortest of time. I accept that in order to achieve maximum leverage for lifting, casting and controlling the line, this is where the right hand should be, *but* we

Two rods, a 13ft and a 15ft. The handles are different lengths, but this does not mean to say that you have to adopt a forward hunched position in order to use the longer one.

Founding the correct grip is elemental if we are to cast effectively.

should not make ourselves uncomfortable. If the body is hunched, the lower back soon starts to object, and when this happens we usually seek the comfort of a warm bath in favour of a river bank!

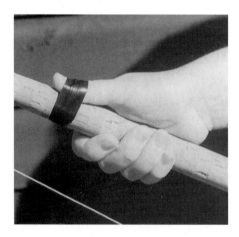

When teaching novices new to the double-handed rod I frequently find their uppermost hand creeping slowly down the handle. To stop persistent offenders I tape down their thumb.

My approach is to tell students to keep their backs straight and to slide their right hand along the handle of the rod from the reel seat until the weight of the rod is supported with the least amount of strain; with most people this position is achieved just before the arm becomes fully straight, that is, the elbow remains slightly bent. The left hand is placed on the bottom section of the handle and helps to support the rod and keep it in check close to the angler's chest while the upstream 'D' loop is being formed and during the execution of the forward power strokes. If the handle drifts too far away from the chest while establishing the 'D' loop, the dignity of the cast will suffer. When taking hold of the rod handle, the hands should close around it from beneath; when closed, the thumbs should be on top of the handle and pointing along the length of the rod. In this fashion we can secure a 'fast' grip which will stop the rod handle from turning when the rod is moved when establishing our 'D' loops and forward punches.

One thing I have learned over the years is that if rod handles accumulate grime they become slippery, and when wet they become very difficult to grip firmly. To prevent this I clean the handles of my own rods with warm water after every day's fishing as a matter of routine. Always dry the cork thoroughly before putting the rod away.

THE BEST STANCE

The stance we adopt while Spey casting is very important. In order to achieve the best balance I prefer my right foot to be slightly forward of my left, the distance being about half to one shoe length. With the overhead cast, this foot positioning enables the angler to follow the natural rhythm of the rod, helping him to rock back with the back cast and forward with the forward cast. When Spey casting, the same footing arrangement allows the feet to remain fixed, something which I believe is essential if this cast is to be performed well; unlike in the overhead cast where leg movement is essential, only the upper body should be 'active' when Spey casting. Also, since we are normally wading when Spey casting, it helps to keep our feet fixed and so there is less chance of them scouring the bottom. And if the bottom happens to be of a gravel composition, any scouring action by our feet may

Whether you are overhead, roll or Spey casting the right foot (if the right hand is placed uppermost on the rod) should always be positioned a little forward of the left.

cause so much displacement of the gravel that we end up losing our footing and perhaps even going for a swim.

Not only is it essential for our feet to be positioned properly, they must also be pointing in the correct direction. So if our stance is one which points our feet directly downstream and parallel to the flow, we will not perform the upstream loop as nicely and as smoothly as we would be able to were our feet pointing in the direction in which we are intending the line to go during the forward cast. By positioning our feet at the same angle to the flow as we are intending to cast our line on the forward cast, we can turn our lower torso through the same rotational plane as our right shoulder when making the upstream 'D' loop. By doing this, the 'D' loop is performed with more style and grace, and the whole cast made much more neatly and easily than it would be if our feet were positioned pointing downstream parallel to the flow.

THE TECHNIQUE OF SPEY CASTING

The foremost purpose of Spey casting, whether it is the single or double version, is to ensure the safety of the angler when it is windy by keeping the fly well away from him or her. It also helps keep the hook point safe, and permits the angler to fish water where a conventional overhead cast would not be possible. When Spey casting from the right bank with an upstream wind we perform the single Spey with the left hand uppermost on the rod. If a downstream wind is blowing and we are fishing from the same bank we would use the double Spey with the right hand uppermost. When fishing from the left bank with an upstream wind the single Spey is performed with the right hand uppermost, while the double Spey with the left hand uppermost on the rod is used when a downstream wind is blowing.

The principal action of the single Spey cast is to place the line immediately

Effectual casting is not solely for the gifted few; with the proper instruction most can accomplish it quite easily. The photograph shows my daughter Stephanie casting on the Spey.

upstream into the mainstream side of the flow from where we are standing and then punch it out again across the river at a 45-degree angle, so that it uncoils above the water like an octopus uncoiling a tentacle. In order to do this properly any slack remaining in the line once it has come to the dangle must be removed prior to forming the 'D' loop. Some might think that if the line is lying immediately downstream from where we are standing there will be no slack: this is often not the case, however. In stretches of water where the current is strong there may indeed be no 'slack' line, but very often the pace of the current in which the line comes to the dangle in, is not sufficiently strong to take away any inherent 'snaking' that may occur. An inexpensive line will, needless to say, have more undulations along its length than an expensive one.

Pulling in the Line

If the line comes to the dangle and does not lie perfectly straight, we must remove any untidiness which exists by pulling in line. Most of the progressive Spey casters whom I have watched fishing wide rivers such as the Dee, the Spey or the Ness do this automatically, very often because they are casting the entire length of their fly lines and need to pull the rear taper back in through the top ring before they make the 'D' loop. In many cases this means pulling in several yards of line. It is no use just pulling in a few feet of line, letting the coils lie on the surface of the water and then proceeding straight into forming the 'D' loop: this will achieve very little, and the process of pulling in line must be executed correctly before making the 'D' loop. After the line has come to the dangle, make sure the rod point is pointing directly down the line,

Once the line has come to the dangle, we start to raise the rod.

The rod is raised to lift most of the line from the surface.

At this point we bring the line round and upstream by scribing a sleeping capital C with the rod tip. Here the rod tip is at the bottom of the C.

The line is still being brought upstream and has still to alight on the water.
Note the rod tip at this point has completed scribing the C, and is being
brought up ready to execute the forward punch when the line alights.

As the line alights, the rod tip has been raised and the forward power
stroke is about to be delivered.

The forward power stroke is made.

The power stroke is almost complete and the line is starting to be punched forward.

The line extends out over the water.

then – holding the rod in the manner used when the line was fishing round in the current – lower the rod tip so that the rod runs parallel to the surface of the water. (The distance the rod is above the surface of the water will depend on how deep we are wading and the height of the individual.) Once the rod is pointing directly down the line, take hold of the fly line with your left hand (assuming of course we are supporting the rod with our right hand) near the top of the handle, and pull it in with one continuous draw until your left hand can travel back no further; at this point clamp it with the index finger of your right hand against the handle of the rod. Now bring your left hand up to take hold of the line for the next pull. The amount of line which will need to be pulled in will depend on the length of cast previously made and the length of cast you are going to make. If the entire length of your

line was cast previously, five or even six full pulls may be necessary; on the other hand if only a short cast was made, or required, one or two may suffice.

Having pulled in the required length of line, many anglers simply let the line which they have accumulated fall onto the water. However, by allowing this line to fall on the surface of the water it will not be shot so easily on the forward cast because of the drag created which, needless to say, will have to be overcome if the line is to be shot properly; this means that more effort will have to be exercised on the forward punch. My own preference when trying for distance is to hold the line we have pulled in in large, loosely held coils in my left hand because it will shoot much more easily; kept free of the surface, it requires less effort on the forward punch for the same distance cast.

The placing of the line upstream, seen from behind.

The line has landed on the water and the rod has been brought up to deliver the forward punch.

Once the required amount of line has been pulled in and the line clamped against the handle of the rod with the right index finger, the rod tip should be raised smartly to the 11 o'clock position. If it is not raised in this way, the length of line lying downstream of the angler in the dangle will start to snake once again. When this happens it is no use just lowering the rod point and simply pulling in some more line, because if we do there will not be enough line beyond the rod tip for us to produce a 'D' loop to enable us to load the rod. For a Spey cast to be executed correctly the rod must be loaded properly, and if it isn't, both distance and delivery will suffer.

Performing the 'D' Loop

In order to perform the 'D' loop correctly, the rod tip should be kept high, at about 11 o'clock, and swung round with a rolling action of the right shoulder until your left arm comes across your chest like the shoulder strap of a car seat-belt. At this point your left hand should be just level with the underside of your right shoulder socket. Once in this position your shoulders will be in an open position. Some casting instructors will insist that the rod is then raised in order to close the shoulders before the forward stroke is made. This approach is textbook casting. (In my previous book *Salmon Fishing on River and Stream* there is a postured photograph of my wife Mary showing what I call the 'position of execution'; it is from this position that most of the beginners I teach develop the basics.)

For anglers to become accomplished Spey-casters and move beyond the realms of 'average' they must slowly fashion their own particular style. Do not be afraid to experiment when it comes to casting. One

The 'position of execution'.

word of warning, though: go slowly, only change one aspect of the cast at a time, and if distance and presentation start to suffer return to the basics and start again. In time, though, all will come right, and you will notice that you are starting to accomplish the distances you could cast before much more easily; you will also be able to cast further. Like everything else it takes practice. I liken Spey casting to the professional golfer's swing: there is no one swing for everyone, because everyone has his or her own.

When performing short casts up to 25 yards I tend to use the accepted closed-shoulder approach ('position of execution'),

A badly executed Spey cast. The forward punch of the line has been made too late and as a result the rod tip almost touches the water.

but when casting distances in excess of this I prefer to keep my shoulders more open. I am not saying that I cannot cast 30 yards or more when my shoulders are closed: I can, but by keeping my shoulders slightly open I find I can achieve these distances much more comfortably. One practice I have seen employed after the rod tip has been raised prior to making the upstream loop is the swinging of the rod tip inshore: I seldom do this. The practitioners of this approach claim it helps to get the line moving, and in this I have no doubts; but in order to get the rod tip moving upstream to produce the 'D' loop, the rod must be stopped and redirected, and the momentum it has built up must therefore be slowed before it is moved around and upstream. In doing this a 'wheel' of line is created, which must be

overcome before the 'D' loop is formed; if it is not, the 'D' loop very often lacks size and as a result the adverse loading effect it has on the rod results in a loss of energy transfer when the forward punch is made.

The only time I start my initial lifting of the rod in towards my own bank is when I have to place the 'D' loop out into the stream opposite me when I cannot place it upstream, either due to irregularities of the bank behind me, or the presence of overhanging branches which could interfere with my line or rod movement; it is a fact of life that a good many pools we fish are not as well manicured as those we see in many of the instructional casting videos. Also, in order to overcome the 'wheel' effect mentioned above the 'D' loop needs to be placed further into the stream. By doing this, however, the angle at which we can throw the line out over the water during the forward cast becomes somewhat reduced. One way of overcoming this is to have a higher rod tip before making the loop, in other words, bring it to the 11 o'clock position. It is important, nevertheless, that on making the loop the rod tip is not *too* high, because if it is, it may have to be lowered just before the formation of the loop so the line can alight on the surface of the water; then the rod tip must be moved upward prior to the power stroke being made. If we have to do this, correct timing of the forward punch is crucial if we are to complete the cast properly.

Note that the more movements we introduce into a cast, the more receptive we must be to the subtle loading changes occurring in the rod. Also, whatever practices you follow when making the 'D' loop, all movements should be continuous and smooth: these will load a rod progressively, while jerky uneven actions cause irregular loading.

The Influence of Wading Practice

Since a fly rod needs the correct line rating to make it work, it stands to reason that the 'D' loop which we form when placing the line upstream must be sufficiently large to flex the rod when it is punched forward against the weight of the line. Like the overhead cast, if insufficient line is beyond the rod point the rod will not deliver to its best capability; when Spey casting the same applies. Because the Spey cast is performed mainly while wading, anglers must find the optimum depth to which they can wade without it affecting their useful casting range. When overhead casting it makes very little difference to what depth you wade, but with Spey casting it can and often does make all the difference, and it is a point that very few writers and instructors highlight in their writing and teaching. The reason for this is that the deeper you wade, the smaller the effective 'D' loop you can create.

Every angler has his or her own depth to which he/she can wade and still cast their maximum distance. I have discovered that

Demonstrating a single Spey cast on one of my fishing courses.

123

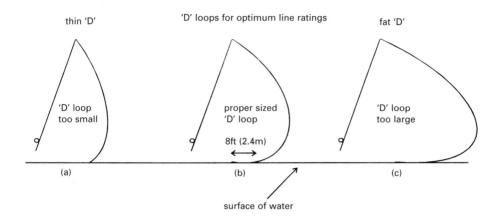

Fig 16 Differing types of 'D' loop: 'thin', 'normal' and 'fat'.

if I wade deeper than crotch depth I lose distance – it is not by any great amount, but there are occasions where if the lies I am trying to cover are beyond backing-splice distance I have had to modify my approach. I have found that if I wade less deeply, even by about 12in, I can execute the longer casts much more easily. Very often when someone is wading and they cannot Spey cast the required distance, the first thing they do is wade deeper, but in doing so the 'D' loop they create will probably be smaller and so will not load the rod sufficiently to shoot the required length of line. If you happen to be a small angler who likes to wade deep, an alternative approach is to use a longer rod; the extra

length will help to produce the correct 'D' loop. Conversely, taller anglers may find a shorter rod more suitable.

Choice of Line

One approach used by shallow-wading anglers when fishing large rivers where long casts are required is to come down one line size; they can then create a fatter 'D' loop than they would be able to with a shorter, heavier line. As a result of this approach, many shallow-wading anglers can throw a much longer line than their deeper-wading counterparts who feel they need to get in even deeper if their casts fall short of the mark.

The progressive angler when fishing smaller rivers where he knows he can cover all the water without wading, will move up one line size; by doing this he does not need to create so large a 'D' loop as he would have to with the prescribed line fitted. Most manufacturers give a range of line sizes, each of which can be used with a particular rod in their range; however, many only give the one line rating. If a range of lines is given I would suggest using the smallest line size when distance is called for when fishing large rivers, and the larger line size when fishing smaller river systems. Generally the middle-size line quoted is a good compromise for most situations, but as such it is not the best for every occasion. For instance, although a rod will perform perfect overhead casts with a line size AFTM 10, it may in fact be necessary to use a 9 and an 11 to cover all Spey-casting requirements.

For many years the standard double taper line has been the first choice for the majority of salmon anglers. Recently, however, a number of anglers and ghillies I know are showing a preference for the purpose-designed Spey-casting lines available from either Michael Evans or Ryobi Masterline. Michael Evans' 'Spey-Caster' fly lines come in two forms: the 'SpeyCaster' has a 25ft front taper for use on small rivers, while the 'Professional' has a 35ft front taper and is designed especially for the more accomplished angler who needs to cast longer distances on larger rivers.

Length of Cast

The angler's height and physical condition – not to mention his mental state – as well as his wading practices all play a major part when it comes to proficient Spey casting. If we produce a 'thin' 'D' loop when we place the line upstream, the rod will not be loaded sufficiently well to execute the cast properly; this will result in loss of distance and bad presentation, stopping the leader from turning over properly. On the other hand, if the 'D' loop is too 'fat' the rod may very well become overloaded when the forward stroke is delivered, in which case the rod will not have enough power to allow the full transfer of energy to take place. As a result of this the leader will not turn over properly and we will not be able to shoot extra line. If our casting range is reduced, it goes without saying there will be fewer fish caught. And if we want to catch fish, particularly on larger river systems, it is often essential to cast over 30 yards.

In order to achieve greater distances it is imperative that the 'D' loop we create is the optimum size for the length of line we are intending to cast: there is an optimum amount of loop for every length of cast, and in order to establish what this is, some experimentation with different sizes of 'D' loops and line ratings must be done. At times when I have given instruction on Spey casting during my fishing courses, I have been asked what distance upstream the line should be placed. On hearing this I cringe inwardly, and wonder if I have been talking in some remote Klingon dialect. The answer to this is quite simple; if the size of the 'D' loop is correct for the length of line we are trying to cast, the distance the line is placed upstream will automatically be taken care of. As a rough guide, the amount of line which touches the water once the 'D' loop has been established should be no more than the length of the tip section plus half the length of the forward taper, which with most lines will measure about 8ft (2.4m) in length. If too large an upstream loop is formed, the line will fall into a crinkled heap. When this happens in a slow- to medium-paced current, a little extra effort put into the forward stroke will help to shoot all the line. In a fast, choppy flow a crumpled mess will quickly be caught by the current, and this is much more difficult to compensate for: the line, needless to say, will not be cast so easily or nicely because the current acting on the mound of line will overload the rod, especially if fishing with anything other than a floater. It is far easier to increase the loading on a rod when committed to a cast, than it is to reduce it.

THE ROLL CAST

When teaching how to Spey cast, many instructors begin by telling their 'students' they must first become proficient at the roll cast. The interpretation of the roll cast, however, seems to vary: for example when I was a boy, the roll cast described in the books and magazines of the time showed that when properly executed, the line rolled out along the surface of the water (*see* Fig 17c); it was also the style of completion taught by the leading instructors of the time. However, somewhere along the way it has gone through a transformation, and nowadays if it does not extend above the surface of the water it is considered wrong. When exactly this change of interpretation took place I am not sure, but I suspect it did so because some acknowledged expert proposed that it was from the roll cast that all Spey casts are executed; so it changed to make it easier to explain the principles of the Spey cast to beginners.

Today the accepted roll cast is performed by bringing the line back across the surface with the rod tip discernibly out to the side – with the cast of old, the rod tip did not move very far from the vertical; this action is similar to that needed in the forward punch of the Spey cast, and as explained above, is why many instructors get their 'students' to learn the 'modern' roll cast. The action of the final delivery, however, is slightly different: with both casts we need to generate a 'D' loop, but the loop when roll casting tends to be very much smaller than that needed for the single Spey. Also, the loop is not founded by throwing line upstream and dumping it on the surface, but is generated by a steady lifting of the rod; the loading on the rod is therefore different.

The line during the initial stage of the roll cast is drawn back across the surface towards the angler; as a result, the 'D' loop remains relatively 'thin', since the rod only goes a little beyond the vertical plane, while the majority of the fly line remains out in front of the angler floating on the surface (*see* Fig 17a). When the forward power stroke is executed, the energy in the rod is directed outwardly so the line can be lifted and 'rolled' out over the surface, and the power which results from the suppressed positioning of the rod is delivered slightly later in the forward punch than in the Spey cast (Fig 17c); the forward punch is not made until the 'D' loop has been formed and the rod and line has come to a halt. Therefore to roll cast the line out over the surface, a fast 'snappy' action is needed so as to generate enough energy for the line in front of the angler to be lifted; there is normally more line held on the surface with this cast than with the Spey.

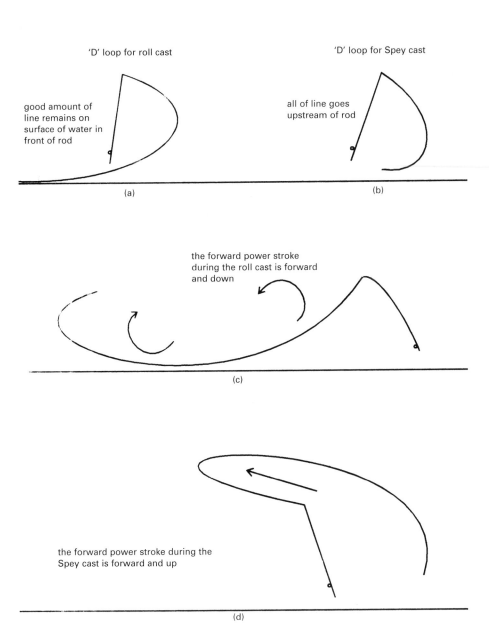

Fig 17 Fly-line positioning when performing roll and single Spey casts.

Preparing to roll cast. The rod is held slightly out to the side when raising it, to bring the line 'feathering' back along the surface. The line at this stage of the cast should not leave the surface.

When the line can be brought back no further the rod should be assuming the position shown.

On assuming the position shown in the previous photo, the forward punch is delivered.

When Spey casting, the rod and line never comes to a complete halt. Almost as soon as the line touches down on the formation of the 'D' loop, the forward punch of the line is made. Unlike the roll cast, however, the transfer of energy during the forward power punch is not applied to the line until the tip of the rod has reached its highest point. By applying the power *before* the rod reaches the vertical position, the line is projected up and forwards (Fig 17d). If cast in this fashion, the line will straighten out over the water and not along the surface. If the line rolls out along the surface, the power stroke has been made too late.

A contemporary roll cast near completion. The loop at this stage has almost completely unrolled.

A single Spey cast near completion. Note the difference in line trajectory between Spey and roll cast.

THE DOUBLE SPEY CAST

The only difference between the single Spey and the double Spey cast is that the line is punched out across the water from the downstream position; in order to do this, the fly must remain downstream of the angler at all times until the forward punch sends it out across the water. With the double Spey cast, a section of the fly-line's belly must be placed slightly upstream of the angler. It is during this part of the cast that many anglers make the first fundamental mistake: they try to create the same size of upstream loop as they would when creating a 'D' loop for the single Spey. Like the single Spey cast, the right foot should be placed slightly forward of the left and positioned so it points in the direction we are going to cast our line. Similarly, any slack in the line must be taken up after the line has come to the dangle and before making the cast.

After the slack has been eliminated, the rod tip should be raised to an angle of about 70 degrees to the horizontal; when it reaches this position we should swing it around upstream until it just transcends the perpendicular. When establishing the upstream loop of line, the rod tip should be kept no less than 60 degrees to the surface of the water. In order to do this on completion of the upstream loop the uppermost hand on the handle should come to just above head height, with the lower hand finishing in line with the left breast. At this stage the rod point should be just past the vertical with a relatively 'thin' loop created approximately a rod length out in the stream just upstream of the angler.

Once this has been done, the rod is then swung back around downstream in the same fashion as used to create the upstream 'D' loop for the single Spey cast. If right-handed and fishing from the right-hand bank, our left arm on completion of the downstream 'D' loop should be coming across one's chest like a car's seat-belt, as described earlier. As this position is reached, the line will stop riffling the surface on its downstream travel, and it is at this precise moment that we execute the forward power stroke: if this is made while the line is riffling the surface, or after it has stopped, the final delivery of the line will suffer. The four most common mistakes I see anglers making when performing the double Spey is:

1) making the upstream loop by keeping the rod tip too low;
2) swinging the rod round and upstream across the body;
3) Creating too large an upstream loop;
4) trying to bring too much line upstream.

If you avoid all these points, your double Spey cast will improve enormously.

SPEY CASTING WITH A SINKING LINE

Spey casting has long been associated with the floating line; however, it is quite possible with a little practice to cast intermediate, slow, medium and fast sinking lines. Most rods will be able to Spey cast both intermediate and slow sinking lines with relative ease, especially when fishing streamy water when the lines have not sunk to any great depth. However, in order to Spey cast medium and fast sinking lines we need to bring the line to the surface, and the easiest way to do this is to raise the rod tip to about the 10 o'clock position and pull in line as you would with a floating line prior to raising the rod. After this, the rod is raised past the vertical to form a small 'D' loop so we can execute a roll cast; this will bring the remaining section of the sinking line to the surface.

As soon as the roll cast has been made, the rod should be raised immediately in order to swing the line around upstream to create the 'D' loop. After this the forward power punch is delivered to throw the line forwards out over the water. The whole exercise, from pulling in the line to the final punch forwards, needs to be carried out at such a pace as not to allow any line which may alight on the water to sink. Any line which becomes drowned will upset the delivery of each relevant stage, and distance and presentation will be dreadful. If we perform the cast in the fashion described, it is often possible to achieve longer casts than we can with a floater; this is because of the small diameter these lines have, and the greater line speed they can achieve.

THE ADVANTAGES OF SPEY CASTING

Anglers who can Spey cast have many more opportunities of catching fish than those who stick to overhead casting. There are places and times on most rivers when anglers who can Spey cast will take fish. whilst those who cannot go without. This is because those who stick to overhead casting are 'inferior' anglers, not because they cannot cast a long line and control its transit across a pool, but because they are only 'qualified' to fish the open stretches of water. However, these stretches are generally heavily fished: certainly there are times when these popular stretches produce bags of fish, but when the going becomes hard and there are few fish about, often the best approach is to seek out and fish the stretches where those who can only overhead cast fail to go. At such times any fish frequenting lies in these places will not have seen a fly for a while, and as a result, those anglers who *can* fish such places are often rewarded for their efforts.

7 THE CURRENT SITUATION

CATCHING TRAVELLING FISH

It has long been accepted that travelling fish, or runners, do not respond to a lure as readily as resting fish. This is generally correct, although I must say that I have not found them as difficult to catch as some would have us believe. There is no doubt that resting fish will take a lure more freely than a running fish, but there are many occasions when resting salmon will treat a lure with the same contemptuous attitude attributed to their travelling kin. One example of this behaviour is when a drought comes to an end and there has been a large influx of fish into the rivers, so that some pools have more fish in them than they do lies. Normally at such times fish will not migrate upstream in one continuous shoal, but in batches of varying size – I have sometimes found a pool absolutely stuffed with fish when a large batch is running, while adjacent pools remained fishless.

An ideal situation, it could be thought; however, normally when I have experienced this I have not found the fishing to be particularly good – in fact it is often quite the reverse, as it becomes extremely difficult to get fish to move to our lures. This is perhaps because there are not enough lies available: all the most desirable ones are occupied and the fish in them seem most reluctant to abandon them; also the other fish which don't have a lie are more intent on trying to obtain one than rising to whatever is being offered. In short, sport normally has to wait until the fish thin themselves out. Usually this occurs when the next batch arrives and pushes the 'resident' group upstream out of the pool; if this is a smaller batch and there happen to be enough lies to go round, the fishing can suddenly take a decided turn for the better.

I have noticed that this behaviour is more typical of resting salmon which enter rivers during the first of the summer spates, particularly when fish are trying to run as far and as fast as they can while the river is carrying extra water. It also seems to occur during late autumn, albeit to a somewhat lesser extent, when large numbers have been hanging around the estuary during the summer waiting for a rise in water; when at last they can travel, by the time they have made their way upriver they have become stale and less energetic as a result of having lost reserves of fat. At times they are unwilling to move far, or to rise through three, four, or more feet of water to intercept a small subsurface fly, especially if they have had to overcome numerous obstacles during their upstream migration, or if the beat is any distance from the sea.

Fishing the River Bladnoch on a falling water.

Choice of Line

As soon as the river starts to clear after a rise and regain some clarity, especially during July and August, many angler's first choice of attack will be a floating line, with one or two small flies fished just below the surface. Over the years this approach has accounted for thousands of salmon to anglers who use this method during the previously described conditions. As far as I am concerned, however, the floating line is best employed when rivers are flowing at their normal running heights; when a river is showing some extra 6 to 12in (15 to 30cm) on the gauge a fly fished with a sinking line can be far more productive. I agree that all rivers are different and that there are times when a small fly fished with the floater will be the only method that takes fish; but there are also times when conditions appear to be ideal for the floating line, yet this only produces the occasional fish. The floating line is most effective for well rested or running fish, but it is not the most productive approach for tired, weary, drained fish that have run far and fast, and which are now taking up lies and starting to rest up before continuing upstream. Once these fish have had a bit of a breather they may rise to a small fly – but very often as soon as they have recovered their strength they will push on further.

On the other hand, if these fish are presented with something 'on a plate' soon after they have arrived in a pool, or while they are resting up, they can often be coaxed into taking. The whole object of the exercise when fishing for fatigued fish is to present a relatively large fly at the same depth at which they are lying, as slowly as possible. Let me stress that this technique is not necessarily superior to the traditional floating line technique: it is an alternative method to be used when fish for one reason or another will not respond to the standard, time-tested, small subsurface fly tactics (*see* Fig 18a).

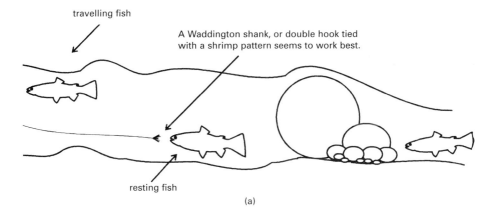

travelling fish

A Waddington shank, or double hook tied with a shrimp pattern seems to work best.

resting fish

(a)

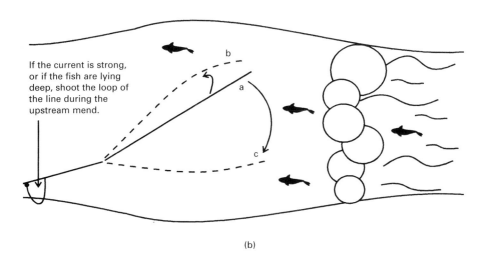

If the current is strong, or if the fish are lying deep, shoot the loop of the line during the upstream mend.

b

a

c

(b)

Fig 18 Resting salmon location and fly delivery in the tail of a pool.

Local Knowledge

The best place to try for these weary fish is in the tail of a pool that has some sort of an obstruction, like a small weir, or where there is a long, rough stretch of water immediately downstream. One such pool which comes to mind is Kenmure on the Tarff; in particular it has a few hundred yards of fast, rough water immediately below it. Not all running fish will stop in the same place for a breather, and water height and temperature will always dictate which stretches are the most likely to appeal to fish wanting a rest. It therefore stands to reason that some pools will hold up more fish than others, and this is where local knowledge has a distinct advantage over visiting rods. The technique I use for tired, resting fish, and with good success, is to present them with a large, shrimp-like fly tied on either a Waddington shank, or low-water double fished with a relatively short leader from 6 to 8ft (1.8 to 2.4m) in length at the end of a Wet Cel ll.

Line Depth and Speed

In order to present our flies at the right speed and depth we must be familiar with the sinking characteristics of the line. Some anglers might think that their line will sink at a uniform rate regardless of the length, but this is not so, and a short length of line cast in a slow flow can sink deeper than a long line in a fast flow. It is therefore essential to understand the sinking qualities of this sort of line in relation to the current in which it is being cast, and also the sinking speed of the length of line being cast at any particular time.

From experience of fishing for these weary wanderers it would seem that the more slowly the fly swings across in front

of them, the better. Sometimes it is necessary to get into the water, or to put an upstream mend into the line in order to get our fly to fish correctly (*see* Fig 18b); at other times both practices are necessary in order to tempt our fish. If the current is particularly strong, or the fish are lying deep, as is sometimes the case, it may be necessary to pull an additional yard or two of line from the reel, and shoot it with the upstream mend. This must be done relatively quickly, however, since the Wet Cel ll line has a tendency to settle into the water almost as soon as it has touched down. Another method is to work out the total amount of line you will require from the reel, but hold back a few yards in hanging loops between your forefinger and the rod handle; now cast just enough line to cover the distance, and then shoot the un-cast loops into the upstream mend.

Yet another method I sometimes employ when working down a narrow pool that holds fish from head to tail is to cast the same length of line down its entire length. In order to control the depth at which the line sinks I will raise or lower the rod point, since the lower the rod tip is held, the deeper the fly will fish; sometimes I have even been known to submerge the tip of the rod if I think my fly is swimming too shallow. At other times I have raised the rod tip almost to the vertical to keep the majority of the line free from the surface of the water when covering a shallow lie. Now and again if a fish is being 'difficult' I will wade in well above it and cast a long line at a shallow angle, letting the fly swim slowly round until it is just in front of the salmon's nose. If this brings no response I will then swing the rod tip slowly back and forth with small movements, from an in-stream to an out-stream position; in this way I can keep the fly swimming in front of a fish's nose indefinitely. I also use this technique for more active summer and autumn fish by making larger sweeps of the rod point; this back and forth action of the fly in front of autumn cock salmon seems to provoke the worst in them!

When maximum fish migration is taking place it is not a good policy to wander from pool to pool, but better to concentrate one's efforts in known resting places; though obviously if you are new to the river or stretch, these places can be difficult to locate. Unlike fish which are well rested, these resting salmon will seldom move any distance to take a lure, and generally when a take does come it is from the very spot where the fish was lying, and is very gentle; there is only the slightest indication that something has stopped the passage of the fly across the pool. From what I have observed, this is because the fish merely suck the lure into their mouths – they seldom appear to move to intercept it. These takes are quite unlike the take of a fish which has followed, and turned back with the fly to its lie.

The Advantages of the Sinking Line

Many anglers will only use the sinking line described above in the early spring or late autumn, believing that this is the only time that they can take fish with it. This sinking line is more versatile than many anglers would have us believe, and those who neglect it in total favour of the floater once the water and air temperatures start to rise around the end of April or the beginning of May, are denying themselves an additional fish or two throughout the season, that might otherwise not

be caught. I have used the techniques described with good success from the Spey to the Stinchar, and have taken fish when others fishing the floating line at the same time retired back to their hotels at the end of the day fishless.

TECHNIQUES FOR DIFFERENT WATERS

In order to try and describe how to fish a variety of pools with different water heights and flows, in this section I shall look at four pools with completely different characters. I will view each pool discussed as 'three-lane highways'. Of course there may well be many more lanes, or even lanes within lanes, particularly on a large river such as the Spey, where one may encounter two, three or even four fast lanes separated by wider or narrower slow lanes, with a succession of boils and eddies of varying sizes situated throughout their lengths. When fishing such rivers some of these lanes may be of no consequence to the angler as they hold no fish, and as a result we may have to wade out into, or beyond some of them in order to cover the lanes which *do* hold fish. What I try to do here is suggest where we are most likely to find fish – which is not necessarily definitive. In each situation I explain with the aid of a diagram how to fish a variety of pools when fishing from the left bank, or wading. Of the four pools considered, the first will have the fastest water near the far bank, the second shall have it in the middle, the third near our own bank, and finally a pool which has two strips of fast water separated by a somewhat slower-flowing section down the middle.

Summer on the Findhorn, a river that delivers good sport with grilse.

Although I will be talking about fast, medium and slow flows, it must be appreciated that the fastest stretch of water in one pool may well be the slowest section in another, or vice versa. Nor does a fast section of water always mean that its surface is choppy in nature: there are many glides where the flow is as fast as any headstream, yet they retain a glass-like surface. Even so, the fastest and roughest section of water in most pools is often found in the headstream, meaning that it is a section of water which is well oxygenated. We are therefore likely to find reasonable numbers of fish in such places, especially during the autumn or summer evenings when the water is on the low side.

Fishing the Headstream

Although the water in these headstreams can be fairly swift and choppy they are usually relatively easy to fish with a conventional down-and-across approach. If they are not, two techniques which are worth considering are the dropped back dropper, or dibbling. Dibbling is written about quite widely while the dropped-back-dropper involves dropping the dropper fly downstream past the fish.

Although it is possible to fish the water with this latter method, it works better if we present our fly to individual fish, and the exact location of the lies is therefore essential. In order to cover a lie properly, cast your line so your flies will fish round in the current in the normal across-and-down fashion; then as they approach the lie, raise the point of your rod until the dropper fractures the surface. Now by manipulating this high rod point, keep the fly scratching the surface about 18in (45cm) upstream of the lie. Keep the fly thus for a few seconds, and then lower the rod tip – the dropper fly will be caught by the current and swept downstream. At times, salmon will make a quick downstream turn and take a fly presented in this fashion without a second thought. Why, I am not exactly sure, but I suspect it is merely an unconscious predatory response by the salmon, brought about by the fly exhibiting a getting-away movement.

Pool 1: The Fastest Water near to Far Bank

In the body of a pool itself the next fastest section of water can be almost anywhere,

depending on the shape of the banks, large boulders, projecting banks, croys, tree stumps and so on. In the slow- to medium-paced pools, like the ones we find on many of the smaller to medium-sized spate rivers, the fastest flow is often down through the centre, not taking into account the headstream, of course. On many occasions, however, and particularly if the river changes its course, the fastest current through the body is often found flowing round the outside of a bend, although it does tend to be relatively calm in temperament. It can vary in size enormously, from just 2 to 3ft (60 to 90cm) in width, to half the sweep of the pool. In order to explain the different techniques I use to fish this sort of pool at differing water heights, I have created three lanes with almost identical widths (*see* Fig 19).

This strip of water on the outside of a bend is normally often the deepest in the

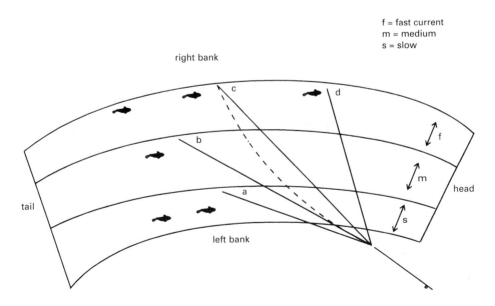

Fig 19 Pool 1. Fly presentation on a bend.

Fishing Pitlochry on the Tay. The photographs show me fishing the fast water down the right-hand bank. At the height shown the fish were running up the edge of the water only a matter of a foot or two from where I am seen standing.

pool, too. When the river is in spate, however, the fastest, deepest stretch of water will not be the most likely place to provide us with sport, and the slower current in the inside bend is where we will find the most fish. Having said this, I know of similar pools where fish will disregard the slowest, most unmistakable flow on the inside of a bend and run up the faster, deeper flow on the outside instead. Fish which run one

such pool on the Stinchar do this: the inside bend on the left bank is relatively tight with a very slow flow, while the right-hand bank wheels round for 40 yards with a good current through it, and it is here that the fish choose to reside, rest and run through. Even when the water is hammering down the far bank I have never witnessed fish in the slower water flowing around the left bank.

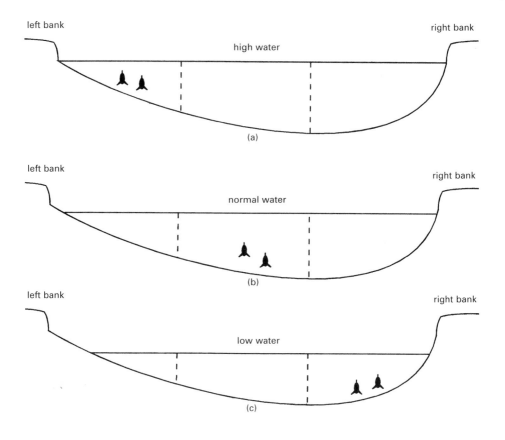

Fig 20 Fish location in Pool 1 for differing water heights.

How to Fish It

Having 'established' my first pool, it is now time to get down to fishing it (*see* Figs 19a and 20a). In order to cover fish which do run up the inside track of such pools it is not necessary to use fast sinking lines: if we do, we will inevitably and continually get hung up on the bottom since the water here is normally relatively shallow, even at the height of the spate. To cover these fish properly we need to use an intermediate, or a floater. The size and colour of the fly will, of course, depend on the height, temperature and clarity of the water. On rivers which run turbid I would opt for something colourful and long, about 2¼in (55mm), while when fishing rivers which remain clear I will fish a drab fly about 1in (25mm) long. There is no need to cast a long line, because all this will do, is cover water which holds no prospect of providing us with fish. When the river is in spate and maximum fish migration is taking place, we must confine and concentrate our efforts in the slow section of water on the inside of the bend. In some pools the best taking place will be right in at the edge, sometimes only a few inches out, while in others it will be where the faster, medium-paced water borders the slower. In Fig 19, the line between the slow- and the medium-paced sections represents this strip of water.

Stripping in Line Since both these stretches of water are very slow in pace, it is sometimes necessary to strip in line in order to keep our fly fishing. From experience you cannot strip in too fast when fishing this section of water – however, do not strip in too much line, but leave enough so the fly can dangle. Even when our fly comes to the dangle and has been there some time, do not be in too much of a hurry to recast; it often pays to keep your fly on the dangle as long as is possible, since the longer it is kept here the more fish it will cover, because it will be seen by resident, resting and running fish. The resident fish will have moved out of the faster water on the outside of the bend and taken up the quieter, *pro tempore* lies on the inside of the bend, where there will be resting fish as well as the transitory influx of runners.

Wading Because of this behaviour pattern it is often not a good idea to wade, because the water in which we will be standing will be the very section in which we are likely to hook fish. There was one occasion when I was fishing a pool I was not familiar with, and had waded out a short distance so that I could bring my fly slowly through the section of water where I thought the fish most likely to be. I had not been fishing very long when I felt a fish hit my right leg with its tail as it swam past. I quickly realized my mistake and waded ashore, and on resuming my fishing from the bank I started to hook fish. However, if a pool is relatively wide with a section of rough water at its head, it sometimes *is* worth wading out a little distance – though take care not to wade too deep. Nevertheless, at times wading can be extremely beneficial, especially when your fly comes to the dangle in the fish-holding area of the pool, as it allows a position from which to work the rod tip slowly back and forth from side to side, to keep the fly moving; then we cover the entire width of the section through which the fish are running.

When the river starts to fall back and eventually flows at normal height, the fish which remain in the pool will take up lies in the deeper middle section of the pool (Figs 19b and 20b). At this time the current through this section, although slower than the current on the outside of the bend, will be slower than the current on the inside of the bend was, during the time the river was in spate. Because of this our fly should be cast slightly squarer than normal to make use of the flow available, and if this is insufficient to bring the line round nicely, I have found it sometimes pays to cast a little beyond the fish and strip in line, or put a downstream mend into the line. When the current is exceptionally slow I will on occasions back up the pool.

At Summer Levels Once the water acquires its summer level the fish will have moved into the slowest, deepest section of the pool, namely the water out from the right bank (Figs 19c and 20c). In order to cover these fish properly in the conventional fashion, if there is sufficient flow, we need to cast a long line to throw the fly beyond the fish (Fig 19 c). The pace of the water along our own bank in these circumstances is seldom sufficiently strong that we need to make an upstream mend to slow down our fly's progress. In fact, upstream mending in this situation would be harmful to the action of our fly and if any mending is required to assist the fly's passage, it should be made in a downstream direction. Since the current where the fish are lying at this time will be faster than the current immediately in front of the angler, any fly line cast across these slower sec-

tions and allowed to drift naturally will not affect the passage of our flies. One technique to use when fishing a bend of a river when the fish are lying at the far side is to try a squarer cast (Fig 19d), and hand-line the fly back so it comes across the fish side on. This technique works well with fish which have taken up residence in the longer-stay lies once the water levels drop back. These fish need to be shown flies in a different vein, because more often than not they refuse to rise to flies presented in the conventional fashion. If a pool has a bend, fish will generally only frequent the deeper water on its outside boundary once the river has returned to, or gone below normal height.

Fishing Channels and Hazards I have noticed that when there is no bend present, the story can be quite different. The Bridge Pool on the Swallow Braes beat of the River Doon is one such pool. The fish which reside, rest or run through this pool nearly always frequent the deeper channel which flows down along the right-hand bank, regardless of water height. The pool in question is not particularly long, about 100 yards, with the most productive part being in the first 25 to 30 yards of water immediately below the bridge. The river here is not wide, with most of the flow being diverted down the right-hand side due to the presence of a boulder about the size of medium-sized family saloon car. Many fish in this pool will take up lies in the main flow of water between the rock and the right-hand bank, while others will lie right up against the far edge of the rock. These fish can only be covered properly by wading out into the quieter water below the bridge and holding the

Not all fly fishing for salmon is done with the double-handed rod. It often pays to adopt a stealthy approach. Here I am using a single hander and crouching to present my fly to a fish in a low water lie.

rod out at arms' length so the flies and line do not get hung up on the rock. Flies dangled along in the strip of water between the right-hand bank and along the far edge of the rock can be very productive.

Immediately downstream of the boulder there is a large dead section of water which is also very productive, but in order to cover these fish properly, the dead water makes the conventional down-and-across approach very difficult. In order to interest the fish here, the best tactic is to cast square across and strip in line, a method favoured by the keeper Jock Woods. A short distance below this the water starts to reorganize and distribute its flow, and here a conventional down-and-across cast works very well. It is not often that three quite different techniques are called for within a distance of 30 yards, but in order to cover this very productive stretch of water properly one must be progressive with one's approaches.

Making the Best of Natural Features
Another pool configuration where the water is fastest down the right-hand bank is when there is a half croy, groyne, a peninsula of jutting bank or a series of boulders projecting outwards at an angle, diverting the flow across and away from

the left bank. This flow will have much more pace than that found on the outside of a bend. (I have shown this pool arrangement from the opposite bank in Fig 22.) The water immediately behind the divergence is usually very slow in nature and because of this, most of the *resident* fish in such pools like to hold up here. Any *running* fish, however, seem to prefer the thin strip of water where the faster current down the right-hand bank merges with the slower backwater section, downstream of the diverting body. Since the fast water under the opposite bank seldom holds fish, most of our efforts should be concentrated in the merging lane. This is best achieved by fishing from the top of the croy, or boulders. Before doing so, however, it is worth moving a medium cast length upstream of the croy.

Once in position, cast your line so your fly comes round to the dangle just behind the croy; if the water is not deep I would suggest getting into it, as this allows better fly control. However, first I would fish down to the upstream side of the croy from the bank, as this section of water can be very productive, especially when the river is in spate and fish are running. The fish which rest up in such lies usually only do so for a brief period of time, and would choose the slower, less paced water immediately below the croy if they were resting for any length of time. Continue fishing, cast and step in the conventional fashion, down to the croy. If you hook fish here, repeat the process; there is no point in moving from a location or modifying your approach if you are catching fish. Only when you have covered this section of water thoroughly, and are sure that this is not 'the' place, should you continue down to start fishing below the croy. Even

so, it may be worth fishing this stretch periodically throughout the day, especially if the river height is changing. Very often a small reduction or increase in water height will bring about a sudden change in resting locations. It could be that while fishing the water upstream of the croy the first time that no fish were present, or the flow through it at the time was not acceptable to the fish. Whether the water is high or low, fish like to take up position a little downstream and to the inshore side of such obstacles.

On reaching the croy we can fish from it, though I would suggest you stay low to keep your outline off the skyline. While fishing from such croys I prefer to cast as little as possible so as not to cause undue disturbance. If you can mount the croy while continuing to fish, so much the better. All we have to do is keep our line fishing down the edge of the current where the two sections of water converge. Sometimes this can be done by pointing the rod straight down the line and feeding out more when and if we want to extend our coverage. At other times if the convergence lane is slow in pace with no pull through it, it may be necessary to move the rod point back and forth in extent to catch some draw from the edge of the faster current to work out some line.

One other method of covering this type of pool is to cast square across into the fast water and strip the fly back, right up to our own bank. And another approach which is often successful is to 'draw' the fly through the two slower sections once it has left the faster current. In order to do this, first lift the rod point vertically until it can be raised no further, then swing the tip inwards over the right shoulder. These actions result in the fly moving square

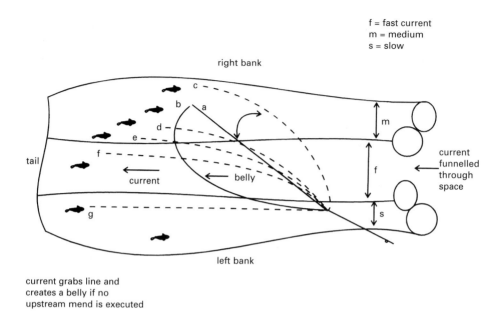

f = fast current
m = medium
s = slow

right bank

c

b a

d

e

f

tail

current

belly

g

m

current
funnelled
through
space

f

s

left bank

current grabs line and
creates a belly if no
upstream mend is executed

Fig 21 Pool 2. Fish location and fly presentation in a pool with a fast central flow.

across the two slower currents and then turning and moving upstream, this change in direction sometimes proves too much for an undecided fish.

The next pool I shall look at is one which has a fast flow down through the middle and is flanked with slow- to medium-paced currents on both sides (Fig 21).

Pool 2: The Fastest Water down the Middle

To start with I will be discussing how to fish this pool with a floating line. With reference to Fig 21, if we were merely to cast our line to position (a) and do nothing, the central flow would create a large downstream belly in it; this is shown by line position (b). The faster the flow, the sooner the belly will be

generated and the larger it will become. On occasions a bellied line can be highly effective, especially if we have covered a fish in the 'correct', traditional, down-and-across fashion and failed to provoke a response. For the best part of the time, however, we must strive to present our flies to the fish in such a fashion as will provide them with a swimming speed acceptable to the salmon for an equivalent-sized creature swimming within the flow.

As soon as we have made our initial cast, we must mend line. The amount of line mended and the position we place it upstream depends on the status of the central flow. If this is not too fast in nature a small upstream mend will suffice, with the body of it being made to land in the central flow; but if the flow is swift in nature, a good proportion of the line in the upstream mend must be placed within the calmer water in which we are presenting our flies. This is shown with line positions (c) and (d). One line mend with a fast central flow will not be sufficient to keep a belly out of the line, and frequent mends may be required to keep the fly swimming properly through the slower section of water.

Once the fly starts to leave the slower water (line position (e)), we will still have to mend line to slow down the progression of our fly, but not so that the line is mended into the quiet water on the far side: the mends now made need to be relatively small in size in order to try and keep the line parallel to the flow. As our line reaches position (f) we may have to hand-line in some line in order to keep our fly fishing – as it approaches the dangle position (g), it will 'die' because of the lack of current. Now, any fish which has followed our fly out of the main flow either from the medium flow on the opposite side, or from the faster central flow, will expect its water speed to increase as it enters the slower inside lane, and in order to promote our deception we must be ready to hand-line. If we are fishing a small fly, the speed we pull in line cannot be too great, but if the fly is large, pull in a good two or three yards at speed. This upstream acceleration of our fly can sometimes prove irresistible.

Using a Sinking Line
Remember that the shallower the angle our line is presented to the central flow, the more slowly our flies will fish. In order to fish the holding water on the far side of the pool properly with a sinking line, we have to modify our approach and place more line on the upstream mend

into the medium-paced section on the other side than we would when using a floater. The faster the sink rate of the line used, the greater the amount of line we need to mend into the medium-paced section, because it is not so easy to make corrections after the initial mend is made, particularly if the line has a fast sinking rate. If the line is a neutral density or slow sinking type, further mends can be employed, meaning the initial upstream mend does not have to be so generous. Unlike a floating line which rides on the surface and only moves through one plane, a sinking line moves through two dimensions: not only is it sweeping across the pool, it is moving down through it, and so it takes it longer to traverse a pool than a floater. The time differential is not vast, but because of this it does enable us to deliver a fly more slowly.

A pool similar in character to the one shown in Fig 21 is Rogers on the River Bladnoch. Its main difference is that it has no dam at its neck, and it widens significantly near the tail as it joins Ash Trees; another characteristic is that it has a relatively narrow neck-stream of rough water which descends with a quite noticeable descent before starting to widen out. The pool is about 100 yards long, and 25 yards wide at it widest part, and the flow down through its centre is quite visible. Most of the fish reside, rest and run up the quieter water on the far side, and the best taking section is between two concrete pillars on the opposite bank. I remember fishing the pool one October when the river was running with a few extra inches on the marker. The weather was mild and pleasant with mixed overhead conditions, and a reasonable number of fish were present, with a steady procession of runners showing

*Fishing the Nut Bank pool on the River Bladnoch. The photographs show
the central current through the pool looking from an upstream and
downstream position.*

down the far side. Having established the water and air temperatures before starting to fish, I opted for the floater.

Although the floating line was unquestionably – or so I thought – the line of the day, I was not entirely happy about the way my flies were fishing, because I could not keep the central current from grabbing my line. Even by experimenting with different size mends executed from different angles, I could not find the speed I was looking for to fish my fly. Something had to be done, so I changed over to a sinking line. I felt that even though I could not control this line with the same ease as the floater, as long as I could create enough 'liftover', the longer time it would take for it to travel the same distance as the floater would keep it in the holding section of water long enough for any fish present to take an interest in my fly.

When I was about eight yards down from the uppermost concrete pillar on the opposite bank I felt the unmistakable draw of a fish – a cock fish of 9lb, as it turned out. It could be argued that the fish was new into the lie and would have taken my fly fished with the floater; perhaps it

would, we have no way of knowing. However, I strongly believe that the fish was already in the lie and came to my fly because I was fishing it more slowly. I am not saying it is always possible to fish a fly more slowly with a sinker than one presented with a floater: this would be foolish, and for most situations the floater is supreme. There are, however, times and places where it is just not possible to control a floating line in the way we would like to, and as a result it often pays to try a different line density. Having said this, although in this instance my change of tactics worked, there are many days when it doesn't seem to matter what I do.

The Beauly Belly
One technique which seems to work well when the central flow is swifter than the flows along each bank is the 'Beauly Belly'. With this approach, the fly is cast square across the current and then left to its mercy, as a result of which a belly quickly develops in the middle of the line. This starts to drag the fly head first downstream

Fish can be taken from the streamy water upstream of the Old Spey bridge, but in order to do so one must know the position of the lies within the flow to the exact inch.

through the slower water flowing along the far bank. When the line is pulled downstream further it will pull the fly round, so that by the time it is in the middle of the central flow it will be fishing square to the current. As the line fishes round in the current it will start to straighten out, and when this happens the fly will turn through 90 degrees and face into the flow. The two most likely times of a fish taking our fly presented in this fashion is when the fly changes direction; that is, just after the moment of maximum belly and just before the belly disappears.

Different Approaches for
Similar Pools
Of all the pool types you are ever likely to encounter, the profile described above is probably one of the most common. Although pools may be similar in character, the fish may lie in totally different places, and because of this a different approach must be used if we are to cover the fish properly. I know of three similar-looking pools on the same river where even during the same height of water, the fish will enter, reside and run through completely differently. In one pool, running fish will enter the central flow at the tail and cross over to the slower, calmer water flowing out from the opposite bank. In another instance the fish will enter the calmer water at one side and cross over into the calmer water on the other, while fish which run into the other pool will enter and run all the way through the central flow. In yet a further pool, the fish enter the tail of the pool in the central flow and then cross over and run up through the calmer water on the opposite side; once the water levels start to drop they will

generally frequent the heavier flow down the middle. Even though each pool appears similar to the others, they are totally unique, and as such they must be fished in the way most suitable for the prevailing conditions.

Pool 3: the Fastest Water near the Left Bank
The next pool I shall look at is one which has the fastest flow near the left bank, with the slowest down the right. The areas shown below the lower of the two half-croys (the one with fish 1 lying in front of it) may not always be fashioned in the way I have shown in Fig 22 , but it is a good representation of the flow distribution one is likely to find below such an obstacle. In the figure I have shown two croys. If only the lower of the two croys were present, the main flow would be by the arrow. If there happens to be a croy upstream of the one in front of which fish 1 is lying, the flow would still be directed down the left-hand bank, with two similar sections behind it as found below the lower croy.

Fishing Round a Half-croy
In order to cover fish 1 properly I would suggest getting into the water to assume a position almost immediately upstream from it; this is so we can bring our flies across in front of the fish as slowly as possible. To do this properly we must cast our line 'a' at a shallow angle, and then make an appropriate-sized upstream mend. The fish which take up lies in front of these half-croys will usually take up position just upstream of the obstacle; I have seen fish lying in front of boulder-

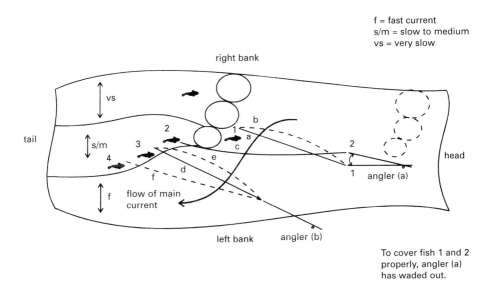

f = fast current
s/m = slow to medium
vs = very slow

right bank

vs

tail

s/m

2

1
a
b
c

2

head

3

4

e
d
f

1

angler (a)

f

flow of main
current

left bank   angler (b)

To cover fish 1 and 2
properly, angler (a)
has waded out.

Fig 22 Pool 3. Fish location and fly presentation in a pool with a fast near-side flow.

made croys with only their heads showing, their tails out of sight in a crevice.
Frequently fish will also lie along the
upstream edge of the croy. It often pays
when fishing above such croys to cast a
length of line that allows your flies to
swing round in front of the croy face with
only an inch or two to spare. I remember
one fish which I hooked some years ago,
a good one as it turned out, that was so
close to the croy face that when I first felt
my line tighten I gave it a few pulls to try
and free it; on the third or fourth pull, the
croy moved!

Before presenting flies tight against the
croy face, it is worthwhile presenting your
fly about one to two yards upstream of it,
as there is every likelihood that there will
be a fish or two there as well, particularly
if the half-croys are made of concrete, or
are filled wire cages and have a smooth

face. Then there are generally no suitable
crevices into which fish can tuck themselves, and those which lie above such
smoothly manufactured obstacles have no
choice but to take up lies either along the
upstream edge, or just upstream of them,
usually by about one to two yards. From
my experience, salmon which take up lies
in front of croys and which come to the
fly, generally turn towards the slower
water – although I *have* hooked a few fish
which turned towards me! All of these
fish were immediately caught by the
faster current and took out some amount
of line before I managed to get them under
control; it only takes a few seconds for a
fish in this kind of flow to have you down
into the backing. I recall one fish of 10lb
which did just this in the 'Below Island'
pool on the Yonderton stretch of the River
Doon. About halfway down the pool there

151

was a croy which came two-thirds of the way across the river from the right bank, and the current which flowed round the end of this was, to say the least, strong (I say 'was', because the croy has since been removed by the owners of the opposite bank). I landed my fish, but not before a fiasco – however, that's another story!

Fishing for Fish 2

When fishing for fish 2 which is lying behind the croy, it may be necessary to wade out a little deeper in order to get our fly line to caress the side of the croy; by doing this, the back force of the water around the edge of the croy will station our fly in front of the fish. Sometimes this is easy to achieve, at others it can be very difficult – it all depends on the currents produced by the croy. When the current is not being 'fisher-friendly' we may have to keep changing the position of the rod tip to counteract any unhelpful currents being produced along the near-side edge of the croy. Sometimes it is possible to achieve the desired means of presentation by holding our rod tip out at more of an angle to the flow; by doing this we can use the dynamics of the current around the edge of the croy to establish a hold on the line.

I have found when fishing such places that a sinking line is sometimes more easily manipulated into place, perhaps because the subsurface currents flow at a slower speed than those found on the surface. These Wet Cel lines have a tendency to sit down in the current, rather than ride it like a floater. Generally, sinking lines are much more difficult to control, but this is one situation where they can be controlled with relative ease. The density of line used will, of course, depend on how active the fish

are, on the water temperature, the pace of the current, and so on.

Fishing for Fish 3 and 4

To present our flies to fishes 3 and 4 we could fish from the same position as angler (a), but this would mean extending line in the fashion I described earlier, when the croys would be protruding into the flow from our own bank, ie the left. Controlling a long line is much more difficult than a short one. When possible and where the current allows, I prefer to fish for such fish from the bank, as shown by angler (b). Initially we should cast our line 'd' so our fly goes beyond where the fish are lying; if we were to leave the fly line at the angle shown, the fast water to the side where the fish is lying would quickly form a large belly in it. Sometimes if the fish are lying in the converging flows this can be quite a good tactic to employ, but the fish which lie in the quieter, slower water often prefer the fly to be presented with a little more dignity. Because of this, once we have made our initial cast 'd', we should make an upstream mend 'e', and this will help to hold the fly in front of the fish for a short while. Sometimes it is possible to keep the fly here by mending further, but this depends on the characteristics of the flow.

Once the current starts to grab the fly line, the speed and presentation of the fly will change, and it is these changes which generally bring about a reaction from the fish. One method I have tried with good success when fishing such lies is to fish with a dropper: I present the tail fly in the calmer section, while the dropper is presented in the faster, and to try and create the proper illusion I tend to make my point fly smaller than the dropper. By using this arrangement I am presenting two flies of different size at the same 'holding' speed within two flows of quite different pace. In addition, if fish are frequenting both sides of the converging flows it allows me to cover them at the same time.

How to Fish Changeable Surface Currents

In relatively well behaved flows the procedures I have described to cover resting or running fish will suffice, when fishing down any pool, but one must always be aware of any changes in current pace and direction. In fact no pool I know has an even, continuous flow from head to tail, and very often there are many places within the pool where sections of water flow slower or faster than the average current present. Usually the slower sections – the boils and the back eddies and so on – are caused by underwater obstruction. However, although these submerged obstructions will cause the flow to have some directional change at the surface, the greatest changes of surface current occur when something impedes the flow by being proud of the surface. For example, a rock which is proud of the surface will create a definite change of flow: there will be a 'V' with a large, dead section of water immediately downstream of it, the obstacle having caused the flow to be wedged apart, and it may be some distance downstream before the split in the current is resolved. The size and shape of the dead water depends on the pace of the current and the size of the obstacle impeding the flow – the larger it is, the larger the 'V'.

When fishing this type of pool, it is – like any other pool – essential to know

A rock cutting the flow as described. The 'dead' section behind the obstruction can be seen quite easily.

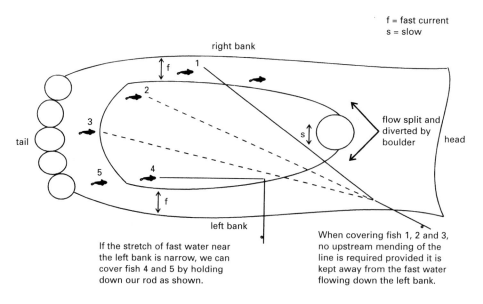

Fig 23 Pool 4. Fish location and fly presentation in a pool with a slow central flow.

where the fish are likely to be at any given water height. In Fig 23 I have assumed the running fish go up the fast water along the right bank, while the resting fish frequent the tail of the pool and the lower section of the 'V'. In fact, this type of pool is not as difficult as one might think. To cover fish 1, 2 and 3 all we have to do is cast a long enough line to reach the flow down the right bank and at an angle of approximately 45 degrees. Provided we keep the line out of the fast water near our own bank, there is seldom any need to make an upstream mend. When covering fish 1, the slow water behind the obstacle will buffer the effect of the fast water where the fish is, and stop our fly from fishing too fast.

As the line comes across fish 2, it is sometimes beneficial to lower our rod slightly and allow some of the line out from our rod tip, so it is caught by the flow where the slow and fast water come together. Do not, however, let the line be taken by anything other than the converging flows; if it is grabbed by the full force of the fast water down the left bank, the fly may well fish too fast as it covers fish 3. This will depend on the size of fly being fished: if it is a small one we must keep its speed in check, if a large one it may be well to let the current grab the line because this will cause the fly to accelerate away from the fish. Provided the speed of the fly does not become excessive, the fish in the slower 'V' section will often follow and take.

When presenting a fly to fish 4 and 5 we can cast a shorter line and work it through the fish-holding sections as I described previously. A more relaxing way to cover the same stretch of water, however, is to hold our rod at right-angles to the flow as shown. This means our fly is always in the optimum taking position, because every fish resting or passing through the lie will see it. A fly which is cast and allowed to swing across the current will only be in fish-holding water for a very short period of its travel, so that fly and fish may never cross paths.

As I have said to begin with, underwater obstacles will, depending on the distance they are below the surface of the water, create oily-type swirls and boils to show the angler that something down below has impeded the flow. In some pools there may be only a solitary boil, in others the entire surface may look like a pot which has just been brought to the simmer. The current in these eddies flows in many directions, and because of this, controlling a fly line can be very difficult. With experience and notwithstanding a little skill, it is possible to atone for two or three variances within the flow when fishing a floating line, but after this it becomes very difficult. When fishing a sinking line we may be able to make one, or even two adjustments if we are extremely lucky or skilful, but very often once the line sinks any distance beneath the surface it is at the mercy of the currents, which in these eddies and boils are not unidirectional and flowing in the horizontal plane, but vertically circulating as well. This means that a section of line may at one instant be caught by an ascending current and lifted through the water like an eagle rising on a thermal, while in the next it has been taken by a descending current and pulled downwards. And since the current within these boils also has a tendency to rotate, the line will be pulled one way and then the other, with the result that we can control the movement of our fly as much as an autumn leaf can control its descent during a gale. If the pool in question is a veritable cauldron,

the line will be fishing at many different depths throughout its length, and 'water command' in such places is impossible.

How to Fish Changeable Deeper Currents

Not only does the surface pace of current vary enormously within a pool, it also varies at differing depths. For example the water behind a submerged boulder will be significantly slower than the water immediately in front of it, and not only this, but very often the water in front of it will be equal to the surface current which is generally where the flow is fastest. Although salmon can be found lying in front of these obstacles, from my observations I have found the majority of fish like to lie either behind or just to one side of them. Occasionally they will lie in front of such obstructions, the times that I have most often witnessed them doing so having been during the summer and early autumn when water temperatures have been on the warm side; perhaps in these circumstances they need the more oxygenated water produced by the faster current. Since it is unusual for salmon to occupy pools with a smooth uniform bottom, the water in which there will be fish will be the sections which contain many currents.

Irregular river bankings can at times create back eddies, a water condition often favoured by salmon. These sections of water generally have a circulating current, which means there will effectively be two different currents, one flowing in sympathy with the main flow, the other in the opposite direction. If the back eddy is positioned along the *right-hand* bank the sympathetic flow will be down the mainstream side, while the opposing flow will

The Findhorn. Presenting a fly properly in such varied flows requires great skill.

be to the inside, nearest the bank. This is because back eddies with the types of flow I have described are created by the bank jutting out into the flow and diverting the current in towards the bank. Salmon which take up lies in this situation often prefer the water nearest to the bank; they will therefore be facing the flow, which means they are in actual fact facing downstream. To present our fly attractively to these fish we must cast from a downstream position, so the upstream current along the inner edge of the bank will work the fly.

Normally a back eddy down the *left-hand* bank is caused by the banking having a recess into which a proportion of the mainstream current flows (in time, these recesses often cause bank erosion because when the river is in spate it will eat away more bank). With these eddies the opposing flow will be along the mainstream side of the current, with the sympathetic flow nearest the bank. These eddies can be fished by casting downstream and fishing our flies through them as one would through a slow section of water. Anglers often walk past back eddies without giving so much as a single cast: those who are so remiss are so at their own loss (*see* Fig 24).

THE SUPERIOR ANGLER

For ease of explanation, all the figures shown in this chapter have had either an even, continuous distribution of current, or three quite distinct currents flowing within each section. In reality, however, things are quite different – there may be flows within flows, and thus additional upstream or downstream mends may be required to keep the fly fishing attractively. At other times hand-lining will be necessary to maintain the fly's water speed when fishing from one section to another. Generally the deciding factor between one angler's success and another's failure is not so much by what he does conscientiously, but the small things he does naturally and without thinking about them, such as a small twitch of the rod tip here and another there as his line fishes round. Although the classic fly-water pools of the Dee and Spey look uniform in character and can be covered and fished with a long cast and single mend approach, in order to manage our fly's passage properly from touchdown to dangle, numerous line corrections at times must be made. The angler who simply casts and mends his line will take fish, but the angler who 'manages' his fly's traverse across the pool by diligently directing the procedure, will take more fish than someone who merely embraces a passive automotive approach.

Stretches of water which have many diverse flow characteristics demand a 'superior' class of angler to those who only frequent the classics. Anglers who take fish regularly from these unsung waters do so because they have erudite rivercraft skills which the classic fly angler seldom needs or has to acquire. Seldom have I found an angler who is at home on both types of river, but those who can 'master' their lines in every flow will reap the rewards. Although a thinking progressive angler will take more fish than someone who adopts an insensitive, perfunctory approach, the naturally gifted local angler will nearly always outfish any visitor.

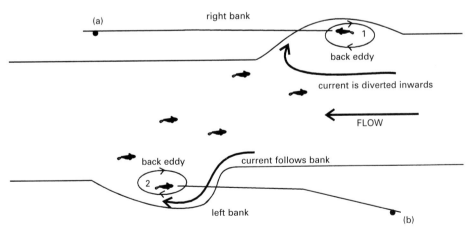

For angler (a) to cover fish 1 properly, he must present his fly from downstream.
To cover fish 2 properly, angler (b) presents his fly from upstream.

Fig 24 Pool 5. Fishing back eddies.

A FLY FISHER'S SEASON

It is now time to relate all the issues we have discussed – fly colour, size and speed, and presentation techniques – to fishing from January through to the end of November. Most contemporary angling authorities when writing about fishing techniques on a month-by-month basis merely repeat accepted conventions, and appear not to have noticed that the weather peculiarities which used to be associated with the respective months have not manifested themselves in recent years. Thus the old sayings such as 'March winds will blow' and 'April showers' have been very much out of place now for some time; from my own observations the weather patterns we expect to experience for the time of year now seem to occur about six weeks late. It could be that these changes are due to the so-called 'greenhouse effect', the reduced thickness of the ozone layers caused by the CFC gases used as propellants in aerosol cans during the 1970s and late 1980s; alternatively the changes could be due to the mass destruction of the rainforests. Perhaps, though, it may simply be the case that we are now experiencing the end of a 'cycle' and the seemingly changing weather is a recurring natural phenomenon.

Whatever the cause, weather patterns *have* undoubtedly changed since I was a boy. I remember when a typical British summer used to consist of one dry day followed by a wet one, and as a result the rivers produced good fishing during the school holidays. How things have changed. Let me give the following examples: the summer of 1993 will long be remembered as one of the wettest on record. Rain arrived in mid-July and lasted for almost a month, as a result of which most rivers ran at good fishing heights until the middle of August; needless to say, this produced record catch returns on a number of the west coast Scottish spate rivers, with an unusually high number of fishing days during July and August. On the other hand, 1994 and 1995 will be remembered as two of the driest, to the extent that during the middle of June 1995 anti-cyclonic conditions dominated the weather over most of the UK. In Scotland this lasted until 7 September, when, having been basking in Mediterranean sunshine, 3in (75mm) of rain then fell in only 24 hours to saturate the north-east coast of Scotland. Further heavy rain over the next four days led to flooding which caused wide-scale damage, with many of the rivers in the Grampian region bursting their banks. Television news reports showed dramatic pictures of whole trees being washed down the Spey, along with the inundation that occurred along the Deveron and

Don. The Deveron rose 17ft (5m), and the Dee and Tay experienced their first major rises in water height in eight weeks. The Tay's 2ft (60cm) rise did not last long, however, because within 36 hours it had fallen back almost to its pre-spate height. Even so, in spite of its short duration, this small rise in water did produce some excellent catches in some of the middle beats; I spoke to one angler who alone took over thirty fish for his week. And as the water level fell back to its pre-spate height, the anglers fishing the town water at Perth started to do particularly well, with some very good catches of fish being made.

Although certain areas received rain it was not widespread, and in some places only flirted with catchment areas so that quite a number of rivers along the west coast of Scotland missed out. Thus while some rivers enjoyed a small rise in water height which brought in the first runs of the season, their neighbours, sometimes only a few miles away, continued to run in a skeletal state; the Ayrshire rivers had to wait patiently until 25 September for any 'real' rain to arrive. But then the River Doon, for example, in 1995 produced what can only be described as phenomenal sport: where normally some beats in a 'good' week would produce fifteen to twenty fish, in 1995 the same beats were producing this number per *day*; one beat alone produced 180 for one particular week, forty-five of them taken in one day. The beat in question finished the season with over 800 fish, where normally this figure would have represented 66 per cent of the total rod catch from the entire river.

Enough of these considerations: I shall now describe a typical 'progressive' fly fisher's season.

JANUARY AND FEBRUARY

Although it is referred to as 'spring' fishing, anglers who venture forth in the first two months of the year are frequently reminded that this is still the middle of winter, and February is frequently the coldest. Since fishing a fly with a long double-handed fly rod is a more dynamic activity than spinning, it stands to reason that it will help fight off the cold!

Choice of Tackle

On some rivers there is no dilemma concerning choice of tackle, as many spring salmon rivers have a strict fly-only policy. The length of rod used will depend on the river being fished: on rivers such as the Tay or Tweed a 16ft or 17ft rod will be the first choice of many anglers; on rivers such as the Spey and Dee it will be a 15ft rod, while on smaller rivers like the Helmsdale or Brora many anglers will opt for a 13ft or 14ft. But whatever rod you choose, it must have sufficient backbone to lift and throw a medium to fast sinking line such as a Wet Cel ll or equivalent, with a long weighty fly, against a strong northerly or easterly gale.

Technique

Although for the best part of the time during the spring the premise is to fish slow and deep, one must always be aware of the physical attributes of the river we are fishing, and very often this policy is inappropriate on many of the smaller, lesser known spring rivers such as the Bladnoch, Cree or Girvan. In these, a fast sinking line would be detrimental, and very often at this time of the year the most suitable tactics are those employed during mid- to late April or the early autumn – that is, to use an intermediate or slow sinking line; though whatever the river you fish, the more slowly you can present your fly to the fish, the better.

One way to accomplish this is to cast a long line at a 'shallow' angle to the flow. If depth is required, you can either take a couple of paces downstream before making the upstream mend, or you perform two mends. The first mend is executed in the normal manner, but with the second mend we have to shoot extra line. In order to do this we must pull a few extra yards of line from the reel before making the first mend; this extra line is kept in reserve by the index finger clamping it against the handle of the rod. On the execution of the second mend, the line is released. If you opt for the two-mend approach, the second one *must* be executed quickly, before the line starts to settle in the water. Once it has settled, the second mend will not be made easily or neatly.

Another approach, especially when fishing smaller rivers, is to wade into the head of the stream – a not-too-pleasant experience unless you are fortunate enough to have a pair of neoprene waders! When in position, hang your fly along the edge of the currents by working it slowly back and forth by moving the rod tip from side to side. Also bring the fly right into the slack water along the edges of the streams. In the very slow water it sometimes pays to slowly hand-line your fly back upstream for a few yards before making the next cast. Very often a fish which has ignored a fly fished across its nose will eagerly rise to one which has been cast beyond it and pulled upstream past it from behind.

When to Fish

The days at this time of the year are short, but this does not mean you must fish hard from sun-up to sunset. Very often the most productive time is between 11a.m. and 2p.m. because this is when the air and water temperatures are most likely to be at their highest. Quite often I have found that it pays to stop for lunch at around 2p.m. and to resume fishing again around 3p.m., continuing until last light; and if the air and water temperatures do not start falling sharply after the sun has gone down it is worth fishing well into the dark, because very often what little fish migration there is at this time of the year will be taking place then. As is usual, a fish fresh into a new lie is often a taker.

Which Fly or Lure to Use

Many anglers who pursue spring fish at this time of the year, especially on the larger river systems such as the Tay, opt for the spinning rod. Certainly most fish taken on such rivers at this time fall to a spun or harled lure; however, a large yellow or yellow-and-green fly fished with equal enthusiasm and perseverance can often provide a springer to two. One fly which is extremely popular on the Tay for spring salmon is a Yellow Ally's Shrimp, and although many anglers only fish a Garry Dog during the autumn, this fly also has a proven record as a seducer of spring fish. Anglers who fish the Slaney, which flows through County Wexford in the Irish Republic, and the Blackwater a little further to the south, have found that a yellow lure such as the Garry Dog and Yellow Belly tube fly are excellent attractors of spring salmon.

Reg Righyni in his book *Advanced Salmon Fishing* (in the section, called

Harling for spring salmon on the Tay. Although this is the standard practice employed at this time, the fly rod should not be disregarded as a means of catching fish.

'The Colour of the Lure') cited similar findings apropos a yellow fly, or lure for spring fish. He suggested that the reason why an all-yellow, or a yellow/green combination is so successful for spring fish is primarily related to how and where these flies are normally presented: this is generally well below the surface at this time of the year, so the background against which they are usually viewed is dark. The fly is therefore seen not in silhouette, but in all its colourful glory, and so will be highly visible against the dimly lit background of the river. (This is the reverse situation of an all-black fly fished high in the water when viewed against a clear cloudless sky.) I must say I find myself in complete agreement with Reg Righyni's conjecture.

Likely Problems

The three main problems presenting themselves to anglers at this time of the year are lack of fish, water height and grue. Grue is that evil stuff which occurs when ice crystals form into larger suspended bodies; when this occurs, all fishing activity ceases. However, given a slight rise in temperature, even a fraction of a degree, it can melt in minutes – and as it disappears the moment must be seized, because any fish present usually come on the take. Very often the only fish of the day which *do* get taken are landed within the first few minutes after the grue has vanished.

MARCH AND APRIL

Regular monitoring of the water temperature during January and February is not that crucial, as a large fly fished 'deepish' in the water will be the only method likely to bring results. Come March and April, however, the situation is often quite different, and disregarding the water temperature could well result in us using the wrong approach when the fish come 'on'. Since it has been established that water temperature plays a significant part in determining salmon's taking behaviour, we will consider how it should be done properly.

Measuring Water Temperature

Generally when most anglers measure the water temperature they merely wander down from the hut, immerse their thermometer, wait a few seconds and then take a reading. Sometimes they keep it there long enough for the 'liquid' to move and hold a new level, but usually the immersion time is wholly inadequate for an accurate reading to be obtained. Mercury, or alcohol bulb-type charged thermometers do not respond to temperature changes in a linear fashion: although the scale is linear, the rate of change is exponential, and as such it takes longer for the liquid to move the last 10 per cent of its travel than it does the first 90 per cent; in fact it often looks as if it has stopped moving altogether. So in order to secure an accurate reading, anglers must be patient and leave their thermometers submerged for long enough to enable the water temperature to activate the thermo-physical changes in the liquid, and allow it time to complete its expansion or contraction. I have seen anglers dip their thermometers

in and out so quickly I doubt if they even had time to get them wet.

A thermometer must also be submerged at the right place and depth to gain the 'correct' relevant water temperature; it is hence important to take the reading from the bottom of the pool and *not* some shallow sheltered backwater, as I have so often witnessed. By taking the water temperature in some shallow eddy, or just below the surface, even if it is in a main holding pool, we will be ascertaining a temperature which will be very different from that which exists where the fish are lying. There have been days when the water temperature taken three or four inches below the surface indicated one size of fly, while that at the bottom suggested something completely different; in fact between the bottom and the surface of the water there are many 'thermal layers'. One might suppose that the closer one gets to the surface, the warmer the layers will become, but this is not always the case and depending on the prevailing location of the pool, and on the atmospheric and climatic conditions, it is possible for the bottom layers to be warmer than those found nearer the surface. Since water temperature directly affects the fish's metabolism, the important reading is the one in the immediate vicinity of the salmon, and not those found in the upper or middle layers. In order to take the *ad rem* water temperature correctly, it is essential to sink our thermometer to the exact depth the fish are lying.

Tackle and Technique

When pursuing fish during these two months there are two main methods of attack. The first is to get the fly down deep and fish it as close to the salmon as possible. This can be achieved by using a fly such as a brass tube, a weighted Wadding-ton or Brora shank fished with a sinking line of suitable density for the depth of water being fished, the idea being that by fishing our flies at nose level to the fish it will encourage them to take. Certainly reluctant salmon will be more likely to take a fly presented in this fashion, but the main problem when presenting a fly deep is that it can be hidden from the fish's view by rocks and boulders; it is also more likely to become hung up on something. As regards improving the intermittent sighting of our fly by the fish at such times, I have determined that brightly coloured ones seem to fair best; it is not so much a 'Now you see me' approach, but a 'Now you can't miss me' presentation.

Having said this, I know some anglers do not like fishing their flies too deeply. It has been suggested that a fish which comes to a deeply fished fly will do so in a more leisurely manner than it would to one fished just under the surface, and clearly the thinking behind this is that any fish which comes to a fly so fished, would not be well hooked. However, this does not take into account the very timeless head-and-tail rise of a summer fish to a small subsurface fly. Whatever you believe, any fish which do come to a deeply fished fly but which do not take hold, can turn away undetected, and the angler in these circumstances fishes on down the pool unaware that anything has occurred.

Casting a fly on the Ballathie Beat of the Tay for an April springer.

The 'Long Light Fly' Brigade

A growing number of practitioners prefer to use longer, less heavy flies tied on un-weighted Waddington shanks, aluminium tubes or long-shank trebles, with the hair tied in long and extending well past the bends of the hooks; these flies are fished with an intermediate, a sink tip or a very slow sinker. Some anglers I know have a selection of braided leaders in differing densities which they fish with a floating line. The 'long light fly' brigade prefer this approach for four reasons: they believe that firstly, by fishing their fly higher in the water, the fish will see it much more easily against the light of the sky; secondly, that if they can keep their fly in a salmon's window of vision for a longer period of time they will be more likely to tempt it; thirdly that a fish which travels up through the water to take a fly will take it much more positively; and finally, that if a fish turns away without taking hold they will see a boil, thus allowing them to cover it again.

Which of these practices do I follow? Well, to be honest I have a foot in both camps, and will employ whichever practice I think will produce a fish at a given time. The lines and flies I use at any one time will depend on character of the river being fished, and the prevailing conditions encountered at the time. If the water is a little high, or there are darkened skies, or if both the air and water are on the cold side, or if there is a cold wind blowing, I will use a large garish fly fished deep with a medium to fast sinking line. On the other hand, if the water is running clear with bright overhead conditions I will fish a less heavy, darker-coloured fly higher in the water, with a slow sinker, or intermediate.

Setting up Two Rods

In order to accommodate the abrupt change of conditions that can occur during March and April, it often pays to set up two rods. When two rods are fishing, both anglers should start off using completely different approaches because it is then a simple matter for the other to take up the method which brings results. If you have a ghillie all to yourself, a rare occurrence these days, encourage him to take up the other rod and fish. This has two advantages: first, you can see which part of the pool he fishes with anticipation (so that you can give it equal attention next time down); and secondly, it provides two distinctly different presentation techniques through the same stretch of water.

The Influence of Water Height and Temperature

Water height and temperature during these two months can change from day to day, as I experienced in April this year (1996): on the 4th (Thursday), the 5th (Friday), and the 6th (Saturday) I was teaching a private party on the Ballathie House Hotel stretch of the River Tay. The day-time temperatures seldom, if ever, reached double figures, yet come mid-afternoon the bright sunshine made it feel quite pleasant and the jackets soon started to come off. As a result of the afternoon heat, snowmelt caused the river to rise overnight, and on each of the three days mentioned we found it running at a different height: on the Thursday morning the water was lapping the top of the Cradle, it was 6in (15cm) below it on the Friday, and 6in over it on the Saturday.

During the Monday, Tuesday and Wednesday of that week the river was running steady, and fresh fish had been taken by either the Cargill or Ballathie rods each day. On Thursday, Friday and Saturday no fish were taken. Another angler fishing at the time thought that the low water temperature, 40°F (4.4°C), was putting the fish off. Perhaps it was; however, on this occasion I felt it was the fluctuating water height that was putting the fish off, and not water temperature – this was not the problem, I am convinced, because there was quite a good number of fresh fish running through the beats. In fact these fish were sporting themselves with the same slow head and tail rise normally associated with running summer fish.

Very often at this time of year if you see trout dimpling or rising to surface flies, focus your exertions on the floating line and small subsurface fly. More so than at any other time of the year, take both water and air temperatures regularly because

failure to detect any changes will result in fewer fish.

MAY

May is considered by many to be '*the*' month for the floating line. I do not agree, particularly as it implies that it is the month when the floating line will outfish every other method. This is totally inaccurate. Probably May has been designated '*the*' floating line month because somebody along the way interpreted another writer's view out of context and as a result merely regurgitated his misunderstanding of it. Unfortunately this misapprehended idea has held firm. What I state now is that May is '*the*' month for fishing for spring salmon with a floater; it is not, as far as I am concerned, the optimum time to fish the floating line. I regard

A large July smolt from the Doon which was reluctant to leave the river. These fish are sometimes killed by inexperienced anglers, who think they are finnock. The fish in the photograph was safely returned.

July and August as being the best months for the floater; during these months we fish tiny flies as compared to the long-winged Munro Killers tied on sizes 4, 6 or 8 long shanked trebles or low-water doubles commonly employed during May.

Often during the first two weeks of May it is not uncommon for cold wintry weather to put in an appearance, and it is therefore not a good idea to be overquick in changing to a full floater. Many anglers are now starting to favour a neutral density line in favour of the floater at this time. Given 'normal' May weather, however, the floating line has no equal for taking spring salmon. Now I am not proposing that it kills the most fish: I am saying that it is the most pleasurable method of fishing for spring salmon. As the weather starts to warm, any snow remaining in the mountains or hills at this time will start to thaw, and water levels will rise once again. As a result this usually encourages the existing stocks of springers in the river to move, and also the remaining spring fish to proceed into the rivers, as well as some early grilse waiting out in the tidal bays, Sport can be particularly good at this time; however, when the water levels reduce and acquire summer level, most fish migration generally slows and the fishing becomes hard.

During the first two weeks of the month the water and air temperatures may well be the same as those experienced during the last two weeks of April, but generally they can become sufficiently high to allow a full floating line to be employed. The fly sizes which are now likely to give sport range from 1 to 1⅛in (25 to 29mm) the equivalent to hook sizes 4 and 8 in low-water doubles. When fishing these smaller flies I do two things: first, I increase the

length of my leader; and second, I reduce its breaking strain to between 12lb and 15lb, the breaking strain depending on the size of fly being used at the time. A longer, lighter leader has two advantages at this time over a short, thick one: the thinner nylon allows the flies to fish better, and also to sink just that little bit deeper in the water. Although the water has warmed I will still fish with the double handed rod, because at this time of the year it now pays to start wading deep and fish a long mended line at a shallow angle. This approach enables me to hang my flies over known lies much longer, something I have found to be particularly successful at this time of the year.

When and Where to Fish

With the evenings starting to draw out, anglers no longer have to confine their efforts to office hours and there is now enough time, even if taking hotel accommodation, to wet a line after dinner. The last hour or two of daylight can be a particularly good time for presenting a fly to salmon, and with the increasing day, May offers the salmon angler the first realistic opportunity of the season to wet a fly at this productive time. As the light starts to go, fish which have been holding up in the deeper, slower pools will start moving quietly into the shallower, more oxygenated streams at the head of the pools. Also with the diminishing light some salmon will take the opportunity to migrate further upstream.

Not all rivers of course fish well during the evening. A number of those which flow from west to east in Scotland have the sun during the final few hours shining directly downstream, straight into the eyes of the fish. This is always a bad situation, whether it is during the day or the evening, but when the sun turns the sky red it seems particularly worse. On some occasions fish will come on the take after the sun has died, but very often they will stay firm. Another problem which can manifest itself during the evening, especially on small, narrow rivers, are shadows. It is not uncommon when fishing down a pool to be preceded down it by your own shadow. Sometimes a shadow will make no difference to fish; however, there are occasions when it visibly upsets them, and I have often witnessed fish move out of their lies to avoid being covered by it. Once disturbed, these fish will not come to a fly, let alone anything else.

With rivers that empty into the west coast the situation is not so bad because in these circumstances the radiated light from the dying sun brings additional illumination to flies, which fish at times find extremely attractive. The one drawback is that frequently you find yourself fishing with the setting sun shining directly into your eyes, and this is not a pleasant experience, even when wearing polarized glasses.

From my own fishing I have discovered that the two best places to fish a pool at such times are the headstreams and the glides at the tails; the middle section of many pools which I fish, do not for some reason or another produce fish once the light starts to go. However, I think the simple reason for this is that the majority of fish by this time have moved location, some into the headstreams, others on into the pool above. Although some of the fish in the bodies of the pools may drop downstream and sit in the tail glide, I suspect the majority of fish we take from the glides at the tails are those which have run up from the pools below. If fish are not running upstream the headstream is the best place to concentrate your efforts; conversely, if there happens to be a good amount of upstream migration taking place at the time, confine yourself to the tail. When fishing during the evening I seldom set out to fish a lot of water but prefer to make my stand at one end of the pool.

One word of warning: do not go to the river with a preconceived approach in mind; always review your choice of position. Even though the water conditions might suggest that fish will be running and that the most likely place of taking them will be the tail, be vigilant – and keep an eye on the rods fishing the pools above and below you: I have witnessed evenings which literally screamed 'tail' to me, only to discover I was fishing in the wrong place when rods fishing the 'necks' started to hook fish. Needless to say I quickly changed my ground.

Tackle and Technique
At this time of the year the air and water temperatures can fall quickly once the sun has lost height, and with clear overhead skies it is not uncommon for there to be a frost. For most of the time a floating line will suffice; however, there are evenings when a neutral density or slow sinker may be needed after the sun has dipped below the horizon. The type of line chosen will depend on the overall prevailing conditions at the time, and very often we may also have to increase the size of our fly periodically to counteract the drop in air and water temperatures. When fishing during the day with a 1in (25mm) fly, if the water and air temperatures remain relatively close to the day-time temperatures,

I will resume fishing with one of the same size. However, once the sun has vanished below the horizon and all colour is gone and everything appears in shades of grey, I review the situation. Generally with each change I will increase the size of my fly by about ¼in (6mm); I have frequently finished the night with one of 2in (50mm) or more tied to the end of my leader.

My first choice of fly at this time is one which has a slender, cadaverous appearance; I do not like bulky, obese flies. Since there is a general increase in fish and insect activity once the light goes I like to present my flies at a quicker pace than I would do through the day. Thus in stretches where normally I employ a mend through the day, when fishing during the evening I will leave my line alone to be worked by the current; when the light goes, salmon do not seem to be so critical of a fly's speed, and will rise with commitment to one swimming at a speed they would have ignored through the day.

Another approach I use, especially if a mist starts to develop and I am fishing with a floating line, is to change over to a neutral density because it allows my flies to fish a little deeper in the water. To start off with I will use an Airflo Glass Intermediate; however, if the mist thickens and the air temperature drops quite noticeably, I will change over to a Wet Cel Intermediate, which will take my flies slightly deeper still. When a mist starts to come down, salmon show a distinct reluctance to come to a fly fished just under the surface; however, they don't seem to mind one fished about two to three hand spans beneath the surface.

Unlike when fishing during the day, deep wading can be extremely unfavourable to

our chances of catching fish in the gloaming. Once the light starts to go, salmon will nose up and rest in the thinnest of water, and because of this it often pays dividends to fish during the evening the very water in which you were wading during the day. Very often, and particularly just before dusk, it is best not to wade and to fish only from the bank. (This practice is not only useful during May, it is a highly beneficial approach which should be used when fishing late in the evening, regardless of the month.)

Come the end of the month, the number of spring fish entering most rivers starts to taper off, and the spring fishing is now over for another year.

JUNE

'Flaming June', as it used to be known, can be a very difficult month for the salmon angler because the sun frequently shrivels rivers into a skeletal state; stones that are normally covered with water in the spring are left high and dry to become thoroughly bleached. Anglers who fish the smaller rivers which depend on rain alone to maintain their levels must be patient, and wait until the summer spates entice the first runs of grilse into their waters. Those on the larger rivers such as the Spey are more fortunate, because snowmelt may well keep the river at a good enough height to enable grilse to run, along with some larger summer fish.

When to Fish

With the longer hours of daylight it is often possible to pursue fish round the clock during June; however, there is no point in this, because for most of the time they will be lying with their heads down and completely ignoring anything that swims past. The two best taking times are during the first and last hours of daylight, and this is when anglers should concentrate their maximum effort, paying particular attention to the broken, faster, and threfore more oxygenated sections of the pools. If the water temperature has been tepid for some time I prefer to fish during the first light of the day, for three reasons: firstly, fish tend to be much more active than they are when the sun starts to go down; secondly, any fish which have run upstream during the night and have come into a pool will be starting to take up lies – salmon new into a lie often prove to be taking fish; and thirdly, because the water will have had time to cool through the night, the water temperature at sundown very often being not much less than that experienced through the day – though it must be said that I only adopt this approach if the weather has been on the 'hard' side for some time.

Tackle and Tactics

When fishing rivers such as the Dee, Spey or Tay at this time of the year I will use the same tactics and tackle to those I employed during late May, that is, small flies fished with long leaders of between 8 and 10lb breaking strain. Given rain however, and a good increase in water height, a sinking line and large tube – the tactics used for February and March – will often reap rewards. June is very much a month for the versatile opportunist who is willing to drop everything in order to be on the river at just the right time. Even so,

it is during June that anglers will turn their attention to sea-trout because of the low water conditions and lack of salmon.

JULY AND AUGUST

During July and August it is the grilse which provide fly fishers with the majority of their sport: next to spring salmon, a fresh-run grilse is second to none on the table. They can be ready takers of a fly, but they can also prove to be very frustrating, and in fact these fish have a fascination for me that spring and autumn salmon fail to achieve. Unlike their larger cousins, they are inclined to run upstream in small shoals, and as a result sport at times can be hectic. Nor do they need much of an incentive to run upstream, and at times will run rivers when there is no increase in water height whatsoever. This activity usually occurs during the first and last light of the day, and when the water is flowing at normal summer height it is not uncommon to see fish splashing through 'thin', streamy runs in water so shallow their dorsal fins can be seen clearly, cutting the surface as they go.

For some reason grilse are restless, fidgety fish and appear to be constantly on the move. It is probably because they are so highly strung that they will constantly pluck at flies, a habit for which they are notorious.

Choice of Tackle

Since the water temperature during July and August generally ranges from 55° to 65°F (13° to 18°C) it is advisable when fishing to use dark, drab flies tied on small doubles or trebles, in sizes ranging from 8

Time for a break and some shade out of the July sun on the Tay.

to 12, that is, 1in to ⅝in (24 to 15mm) in length. Some of the patterns most commonly employed are Stoat's Tail, Silver Stoat and Black Pennell, and for best results these should be fished with light leaders of 6 to 10lb and a floating line. I prefer a leader of 8lb, although on occasions I will drop down to 6lb.

A number of anglers – including myself from time to time – like to fish with a dropper when after grilse. There are several ways you can set up your two flies, one is for both flies to be the same size, tied on the same style of hook; another is for both flies to be of different sizes and tied on dissimilar hooks, generally a double and a treble – some anglers will fish the treble on the tail with the double on the dropper, while others will use the reverse

set-up. My own preference is for the treble to be on the tail, because I feel this helps anchor my leader and allows both flies to fish just a little bit deeper. Several anglers I know when fishing a dropper will put a garish fly on the point with a darker, drabber one tied to the dropper, because they like to fish their flies in a fashion that simulates a chase, ie one entity chasing another; they believe that any fish seeing them will want to become involved and that its reaction will be to intercept one or the other.

Incident on the Stinchar

I recall one incident in late August when I had booked a day on a stretch of the River Stinchar. The Stinchar is a delightfully productive river, but it does have a tendency to rise and fall fast, in fact I have known it to be fishable in the morning, yet too low by early evening. On this occasion it looked good as I caught sight of it through the odd roadside clearing, and it was even more reassuring to see that it was running with about nine extra inches on the marker as we pulled the car up at the hut. Since it is not very wide I tackled up with a 13ft 6in double hander with a double taper AFTM 10 floater; I felt this outfit would give me better control of my line and flies. Often when fishing at this time of the year I like to hold the rod out with the rod point at right-angles to the bank because this allows me to hang my flies above the lies. Once I think the fish have seen enough of them, I then swing the rod round so the point runs parallel to the bank from which I am fishing. This action generally excites fish into taking just as the fly accelerates away – why, I am not really sure, but I think it has something to do with the 'getting away' aspect.

The water on this occasion was starting to clear and fall, so I selected a small Silver Stoat's Tail tube fly, along with a small, tatty-looking red hairwing tied on a size 10 low-water double. Initially I tied the Stoat's Tail tube to the dropper and the tatty red hairwing to the point, but after a few casts I swapped them around. I must admit that I don't generally fish with a dropper when a river is carrying additional height and colour, but on this occasion it looked and felt right. And since the pool at the hut generally produces fish at the height of water I was fishing, I saw no point in going walkabout in order to find a taking fish, being quite convinced that any taking fish would come to me; I thought it only a question of time before I

found myself connecting with one, as a steady procession of fish showed as I fished down the pool.

Directly opposite the hut the pool widens and slows, and there is a slow back eddy on the far side due to some bank erosion; covered by a canopy of branches, this eddy looked just right. As I made my way down I caught sight of a fish's back just in the edge of the slack water where the eddy began, so as I reached the spot I made a cast over it: no response, so I cast again – and, the line jumped off the water and went tight. I then felt the weight of the fish and soon realized it was no diminutive grilse as it turned and ran towards the tail of the pool. After ten minutes of short runs and surface splashing it was netted, a fine salmon of 16lb. It had taken the small Stoat's Tail tied on the point.

Tactics for Grilse

Waddington shanks between ⅜ and ⅝in (10 and 15mm), dressed lightly and armed with a small Partridge outpoint treble, are very effective lures for grilse. Shrimp patterns are also very good tempters, especially if fished fast and presented 'square on'. And although these flies with their long tail feelers throw all accepted fly size theories out of the window, they are extremely effective for summer salmon and grilse. When fishing for grilse during the summer when the water is flowing at its normal height, concentrate your efforts in the faster runs and streams. Although the small flies we are using may be out of place in such a fast stream, grilse for some reason do not seem bothered if a fly is not fishing at the 'correct' speed, and in my experience these fish will happily take a small fly fished over-fast, and with great conviction. Perhaps most angling writers over-emphasize the importance of fly speed; I must confess I am inclined to do so myself. At times it is important, but during the summer, fish, and particularly grilse, seem to pay little or no attention to whether a fly has the 'correct' speed or not.

I remember one incident regarding a contrived increase in fly speed, which occurred during the summer of 1995. This was the driest summer since records began, and by the end of July it had reduced most rivers to a trickle. Fishing as a guest on the first freshwater holding pool of a local river, I took a 5lb grilse. When I first saw it, the fish could be seen in the lie quite clearly, but it steadfastly refused to move or to rise to my 'baby'

Allys; since the water was so low and clear I was using my single-handed rod. I then decided to try a completely different approach, so I removed the 'infant' and replaced it with a large red one, which on reflection must have been all of 2½in (63mm) long, casting it a good 2 yards upstream and a little beyond where the fish was lying. As it started to sink I stripped in line to bring it square across the nose of the fish, and when it approached I saw the grilse rise through the water and turn away, flashing its silvery flank as it did so. I tried again, except this time I stripped faster. Up it came again, but it still lacked commitment. On the next cast I stripped in line *furiously*, and this time it took it. I saw the fly approaching from the side, the fish rise

In July it is often necessary to use a single-handed rod, especially when the river is running low. Here I am trying for a summer fish from the Doon.

*When the river is low, it normally pays to fish the fast streamy oxygenated
water below a weir.*

and open its mouth, and then turn away with it – a truly wonderful experience. The fish I am sure must have come into the pool within minutes of me arriving to fish it because it was bright as fresh paint and smelling of the sea, and had over twenty long-tailed lice attached to its flanks.

Fishing Fast-flowing Water

When a river runs low during July and August, salmon and grilse will often frequent fast-flowing, narrow channels of water which normally they would avoid. Many of these stretches carry a terrific

pace of water and are often deepish in nature, and to fish them properly a floating line and lightweight fly is of little use: a heavyweight fly fished along with a sinking line must be used to get the fly down at nose level with the fish. If we can get in above the flow we need only cast our line once, and when we have done so we must hold our rod parallel to the flow so that we can fish our fly in the position of dangle. After a time we can move the rod tip in and out, to bring our fly swinging across the nose of any fish which might happen to be there; with careful manipulation of the rod tip this movement

July on the Tay at Benchil. Even though the water may be low, at such times the double-handed rod needs to be used on wide rivers in order to cover the water.

can be maintained almost indefinitely. If it fails to bring about a response, try raising the rod tip to bring the fly to the surface, and when it gets there, let the waves bat it about; a fly behaving thus will often bring about a Polaris-type response from a fish.

After we have fished a belt of water we let the current extend the line downstream simply by pulling some line off the reel. It is often possible with this approach to fish our fly all the way down a run – in fact with some practice it is also possible to work out and fish an entire length of fly line.

When fishing the faster, streamier sections of water it is also worth trying an over-large fly for the conditions; a garish one cast square across and stripped back at speed seems to do best, and this approach will often bring about a response from fish that have refused a smaller fly fished in the conventional across-and-down fashion.

Grilse as Bad Takers

Grilse have the reputation of taking hold of flies badly, but in fact I have not really found this to be the case. Most anglers I know who complain about grilse being bad takers feed slack line when they feel a fish take, and to my mind this is a mistake when fishing for grilse, which display all the characteristics of hyperactive children – they are never settled and continuously on the move, and I think perhaps it is *because* they are so unrestful that they are inclined to snap at flies in a trout-like fashion. Grilse from my experience are not *bad* takers, they merely take a fly differently, and because they tend to have this fast, trout-like take I prefer to lift my rod against any offers which may happen to come my way. I use this approach throughout the year for salmon, as well.

Basically, I see no sense in feeding slack line to a fish that has taken my fly into its mouth and given it a sufficiently hard pull for it to register at the rod tip.

Rod Choice

On classic or medium-sized rivers it is best to use a double-handed rod. On the smaller, rain-dependent spate rivers during a spate I would opt for a double-handed rod, sinking line and garish flies ranging from 1½ to 2½in (40 to 63mm), the size and garishness used depending on the height and colour of the water. As the water clears and falls to its normal level, I will change to a single-hander and use flies in the patterns and sizes I mentioned previously, ie Stoat's Tails and so on.

The Trailed Tail-fly

A method that works well during these two months is the 'trailed tail-fly', particularly on the small rivers that flow quickly through rocky gorges and have a generous amount of fast streamy water, such as the Findhorn, or the Shin. It is a method to use when more orthodox methods have failed. The method of fishing is similar to the dibbled dropper, but instead of employing two flies we use only one; for best results a fly bigger than 2in (50mm) should be used, tied on either a plastic tube or a Waddington shank.

There are two ways of fishing the 'trailed tail-fly': the first is to cast the fly across the streamy water and raise the rod point to a level that causes the fly to drag on the surface as it swings across the pool; when it approaches a lie which is known to hold fish, work the rod tip from side to side. By doing this we can dance a fly above a fish indefinitely, and it is a method of attack which will sometimes provoke an otherwise unresponsive fish into taking. Both this and the more orthodox approach is to use a fly tied on a plastic tube. Alternatively we can cast our fly across the pool and then after it has alighted, raise the rod point to such a height that it brings the fly to the surface. It should then be raised further so that only the hooks come into contact with the top of the water, and the fly 'trailed' a short distance across the surface. After a short travel the rod point should be lowered and then raised, which will first sink, and then draw the fly back towards the surface between each 'trailing', and the whole procedure is repeated until the fly completes its traverse of the pool. For obvious reasons, when using this approach a fly dressed on a Waddington shank is better suited to one tied on a plastic tube.

SEPTEMBER

September can be either a very bad or a very good month for the salmon fly fisher. I have known years when September in Ayrshire came and went without producing so much as a drop of rain, and as a result rivers ran well below summer level. September 1995 was particularly dry, and beats on the Stinchar at this time which normally have around 150 fish for this time of the season had fewer than twenty in their books. Day-time temperatures for the week beginning 18 Sept were nudging 66°F (19°C), with night-time temperatures of 50°F (10°C). Indian summers do nothing to provide the angler with sport, nor do they allow fish access into the rivers, which is of much greater significance.

Generally, however, and given rain, September can provide some of the best sport of the season, with the bulk of the autumn runs starting on many rivers.

The Importance of Air and Water Temperatures

On Saturday, 23 September, my wife Mary, and myself were fishing the Tay a few miles upstream from Dunkled. The water and air temperatures on this occasion were 56°F and 58°F (13.3°C and 14.4°C) respectively when I measured them around lunch-time. During the afternoon, infrequent heavy squally showers arrived and the air temperature fluctuated rapidly up and down: in between the downpours it rose noticeably and it became pleasantly warm, and on measuring both the air and water temperatures at such times the air was warmer than the water. Come the squalls, however, and the air temperatures took a distinct dip, dropping almost to that of the water. I have never experienced good salmon fishing in such conditions, and this day was no exception. Salmon will take a fly, or any other lure relatively well when it is windy and wet, but only if the air temperature remains settled. I have taken fish when the wind has been breaking branches off the trees and the rain has been horizontal, but this has only happened when the air temperatures remained stable and higher than the water.

Tackle and Tactics

With shorter days and longer hours of darkness the rivers start to cool, as a result of which the fish generally become more active. This is a very good thing as far as the angler is concerned, as it often means fish which were reluctant to come to our flies during the dry, sultry days of July and August are now more willing to respond. In addition, male fish are starting to turn red and become aggressive as they become sexually mature. An all-red fly, or a fly containing red, such as a Garry Dog, will do very well at this time. When fishing the larger rivers with normal water levels we can use the same tackle and tactics as we did in May, in other words floating lines and flies ranging in size from 1 to 1¼in (24 to 29mm) – that is, hook sizes 4 to 8 in low-water doubles. But if the water height, temperature or clarity of the water changes, then we may have to abandon the floater and go over to the sinker and fish with larger, brighter-coloured flies, their size and garishness depending on the temperature, height and clarity of the water. On the other hand, if drought occurs we may well be back to fishing a single-handed rod and the same tiny wisps of flies that we used in June and July.

Wiggling the Rod Tip
One method employed by many anglers at this time of the year, and particularly those who fish the smaller spate rivers, is to wiggle the rod tip. Some angling writers maintain they see no purpose in doing this, but to my mind they are simply confirming how little they understand the extent to which moving water can hold a line and generate life into the fibres which make up their flies. They say that with a long line, the fly will hardly move at all, and if the line is not lying straight then a small up-and-down movement of the rod tip will not be enough even to remove the

kinks in it. In these circumstances I would be bound to agree that nothing would be gained from wiggling it. But if the line is neat and true and without kinks, then wiggling the rod tip *will* work the fly. Certainly it cannot be done haphazardly, and merely wiggling the rod tip up and down will do nothing to encourage fish to take our fly. In order for this movement to be effective, the rod tip must be lifted when the current has the maximum pull; in other words, the angler must be aware of the current working the fly at the time. Once this force is felt, lifting the rod tip will make the fly move forward in the flow, causing the fibres making up the wing to compress along its body. Once the fly has moved upstream by about 12in (30cm), the rod point is lowered to allow it to fall back in the current, and when this happens the fibres in the wing will open out; the two movements are very similar to that of a swimming squid.

Many anglers find that wiggling the rod at this time of the year is very productive. Although it is a practice more commonly applied by the doyens of the smaller river systems, it should not be frowned upon by those fishing larger rivers. No method which succeeds in presenting a fly in a more lifelike fashion should be scorned, especially if fish have refused to move to a fly fished with the traditional approach. Nor is it a method which should be confined to September, because it works well throughout the autumn.

The Sensitive Angler
September is a transitional month, and as a result the angler must be attentive to any changes in air and water conditions; to disregard any changes in these will nearly

always result in him departing the river fishless. The angler who can identify these changes, and who modifies his approach to suit, will enjoy some of the best sport of the season.

OCTOBER

Come October, many of the famous highland rivers have closed. Nevertheless there are still a great many rivers which remain open: rivers such as the Annan, Earn, Nith and Tweed are places many anglers dream of fishing, although access to their more famous autumn beats is very difficult to acquire at this time. Not to be outdone, many of the smaller spate rivers are now starting to come into their own.

Tackle and Tactics

These will depend on the river being fished, the air temperature, water temperature, water height and water colour. If for example, you are fishing a river such as the Annan or the Nith and it is flowing with an extra 2ft (60cm) on the gauge and coloured, the order of the day will be a 15ft rod, a medium to fast sinking line with a short 4ft leader of 18 to 20lb nylon, along with a relatively weighty 2 to 3in (50 to 75mm) fly. However, if they are running at normal height, the first choice of many anglers will be a 13ft rod with a floating line, a 10ft leader of 10 to 12lb, with a Garry Dog or Willie Gunn tied on a size 6 double or treble. If fishing a spate river falling after a spate, we will probably choose a 13ft rod, a medium to fast

An early October fish putting a fine bend into the rod.

The moment of decision. To return or keep?

sinking line terminated with a short 4ft leader of 18 to 20lb with a 2in (50mm) brass tube or Waddington. If these rivers are running at normal height, many will be unfishable due to the lack of water; but for those which still have any semblance of a flow and which have stocks of fish in the pools, a single-handed rod of 10ft with a floating line, a 10ft leader of 6 to 8lb and a Stoat's Tail will be the most suitable tackle for the conditions.

It is interesting that so often when you pick up a monthly fishing periodical with an article on fishing for autumn salmon you will probably read something like the following: 'I attached a 2in brass tube to a short 4ft length of 20lb nylon which was connected to the end of a Wet Cel ll. As the line landed I pulled a few extra yards

from the reel and made a large upstream mend, quickly followed by another. I was happy fishing in this fashion because I knew that by employing large upstream mends and feeding extra line it would allow my fly to get down deep before it came across the lie.' If I had caught a fish for every time that I have read words like these, I would be a happy man!

October Idiosyncracies

October can see the full gamut of weather conditions. I have fished when it has been so cold the fly lines where freezing in the rod rings, while at other times I have been fishing with rolled-up shirt sleeves as I would be doing during July and August. October 1995 broke two records: it went down as the warmest and the wettest since records began, and as a result the water temperatures remained warm enough on many rivers for a full floater to be used; although on others, the water height dictated a sinker along with a large fly. Because of the uncertainty I used a Wet Cel Intermediate for most of my fishing during the month. In fact October can be a fickle month altogether, and it is not uncommon to use lines ranging from a fast sinker to a full floating in one day. On more than one occasion the water temperature when starting out has been warmer than the air, a condition which I have found from experience seldom encourages fish to take well – though sometimes a fish can be moved by fishing a large fly right down at nose level. However, it is important to monitor the temperatures relatively frequently, as I have experienced days when the air temperature rose above that of the water very

quickly and as soon as this happens, a revaluation of the tactics being employed at the time will have to be made.

If the water is running coloured, it may well be best to stick to the sinking line and longish fly – on the other hand, a smaller fly fished higher in the water may be best. There is really no hard-and-fast rule regarding tackle, as a great deal will depend on the river in question and this is where experience of its individual characteristics is worth a dozen angling books. If the water temperatures remain relatively warm, it often pays to keep the Waddingtons and large tubes along with the fast sinking lines in the fishing bag. When the water is warm with not too many extra inches on the gauge, I will start off using small flies fished just under the surface, but come lunch-time if I have had no positive response, I will change to a sinking line and a large fly.

When tying on a fly or making up a leader, do it yourself. Do not entrust these important tasks to anyone else.

When fishing during October I like to opt for a red-, orange- or yellow-coloured fly. Sometimes, however, depending on the freshness of the fish around at the time and the amount of leaves in the water, I will favour a fly which contains all three colours. I have found that a fly containing more than one colour seems to work best when there are many leaves about, and a self-coloured fly when the river has very few. Perhaps the reason for this is that the three bright colours – the red, orange and yellow – being so close together stands out amongst the assortment of decaying foliage.

Shrimp flies at this time of the year are often overlooked, but they shouldn't be. I have found that autumn fish will take a shrimp fly with great commitment, and very often I have taken the only fish of the day on an 'Ally's' or something similar, when others fishing at the time with more 'autumny'-type flies have finished the day with a 'Findlay' (a blank).

NOVEMBER

Come November, only a few river systems remain open, and at this time of the year many of the fish running through them them are well past their best. In saying this however, many rivers such as the Annan, Nith and Tweed will still be bringing in good numbers of fresh fish bearing sea lice, and it is these true, hard-fighting autumn fish which attract the anglers. It is at this time of the year that many rivers will see runs of the larger multi-sea-winter fish. Even so, one must still remember that although fresh run and silver in body, these fish are sexually mature with well developed eggs and milt. Some fish known as

greybacks will enter a river on one spate, spawn, and return to the sea on the next.

It has been said that some of the fish which run on these late autumn spates are early-running spring fish, and I am inclined to think that there must be some spring fish running upstream at this time: however, it is impossible to determine numbers to any extent. Perhaps these early-running spring fish are caught more frequently than we think, and it is simply a case that those who catch them simply label them as autumn stock. However, when these fish are cleaned and gutted they should be easily identifies as springers, because they will have very tiny ovas, or milt sacs. I have heard of other anglers taking early-run spring fish during late November, but I myself have never taken any. At this time of the year, stale, gravid fish which are on the verge of spawning will take a fly, or any other lure for that matter with a freeness which is seldom exhibited early in the season. As a result of this lack of restraint, it is all too easy for unprincipled anglers who care nothing for the future of salmon stocks to gratify themselves with large catches of fish which should be left in peace to be able to get on with nature's business of procreating the species.

Tackle and Tactics

November in my part of the country has a tendency to be a dry month, but given rain, and especially if the summer and early autumn months have suffered a drought, good numbers of fish rocket upstream at this time. However, even though the river may be in fine order one day, if an overnight frost occurs it may well be back down to summer level the next. This does not create too much of a problem in the larger river systems, as they usually still carry enough water to remain fishable; all it does is slow down the progress of the fish. But in the smaller spate rivers which receive runs of fish at this time, frost can bring sport to an abrupt halt. It is not uncommon at this time of the year when fishing a river such as the Annan, Nith or Tweed with an additional 2 to 4ft (60 to 120cm) on the gauge, to be fishing in a similar fashion as one would be during the months of February and March. If faced with such water heights we would use garish flies up to 3in (75mm) in length tied on either tubes, Waddingtons, Brora shanks or long-shanked trebles, the type used depending on the prevailing conditions at the time. In order to fish heavy flies properly, one needs to use a short 3 or 4ft (90 to 120cm) length of 20 to 25lb monofilament. On the two rivers mentioned, these flies can be fished with either a Wet Cel ll sinking double taper line, or a shooting head.

The Shooting Head

Many anglers fishing larger rivers at this time of the year now tend to favour the shooting head. These lines usually consist of 15yds (13m) of forward taper spliced to a shooting braid. Shooting head lines can be purchased ready-made, but many anglers prefer to make their own. Those who opt for shooting heads in favour of a double taper do so because they tend to sink faster and give greater water coverage; although in saying this, they do have a number of disadvantages compared to a double taper. Often false casting is necessary with a shooting head to effect the appropriate line speed to throw it out across the water. Another disadvantage is that once cast, they cannot be controlled to

the same degree – that is, they cannot be mended to slow down the sweep of the fly. In order to fish with one of these lines it is necessary to have sufficient room behind for the back cast. Needless to say, these lines are not suitable for Spey casting.

Choice of Fly

Although a sinking line is the first choice for many anglers fishing at this time, it is not essential to pursue these late-running autumn fish with a fast sinking line, especially when the river starts to fall away after a spate. Autumn fish are much more active than their spring cousins, even when the water is cold. Sit beside a pool at this time of the year and you will see fish sporting themselves regularly, and bow waves caused by fish chasing other fish around the pool. These fish can be taken on a small fly, but very often a large fly is best, even if the water is low, or on the warm side. A large fly such as a red Ally's Shrimp at this time of the year seems to bring out the worse in them, perhaps because being red and therefore the same colour of the spawning livery of the cock salmon, the fish feel threatened. A long-winged red fly will often bring about a response where a small drab fly fails.

Although the fly for best effect should be large, it is best to keep it relatively weightless in design; and do not use heavyweight brass tubes or Brora shanks fished at the end of a fast sinking line if the river is running low – in this situation it is best to use small trebles or low-water doubles with long flowing wings, fished with either a floating or neutral density line. If you use deeply sunk flies you could end up foul-hooking fish, and this is something which even if it occurs accidentally, will bring cutting looks of suspicion.

Appendix I
FLY WINGING MATERIAL

Since anglers started to bind bunches of feathers and hairs onto hook shanks, very few birds and animals have escaped having their jackets used at one time or another. Today there are many different materials available to the fly tyer: as well as several varieties of natural hair, there is a wide assortment of synthetics which can be used on their own, or in conjunction with natural hair to enhance a fly's attractiveness. I include here a list of the more popular materials, and give examples of how and where each can be put to good use.

White Arctic fox tail An excellent material for both salmon and sea-trout flies. It has much more mobility and density than either bucktail or squirrel tail. Being soft it can be used in the slowest of flows.

Black bear hair A very long black hair which is most suitable for tying large Waddington and tube flies. I have also known a few strands be used with some success for tying Collie Dogs.

Bucktail This is usually from the tail of the whitetail, or Fallow deer. In its natural form it is brown on top and white underneath. It is a relatively stiff hair which needs a good flow to make it work. The hairs are fairly easy to dye, and as a result are available in a variety of colours. As

well as this they have a great many hairs up to 5in (12cm) long. They are not, however, really suitable for tying small flies, but are best employed for tying larger flies, ie size 6 and greater. They are also one of the best materials for using on Waddingtons and tubes. Among all the materials available to the fly dresser, bucktail is probably the most common hair used in modern hairwing salmon flies.

Calf tail Calf tail hair is relatively short and semi- translucent. It comes in useful lengths of between ½in (12mm) and 2in (50mm). It is, however, coarser hair than squirrel, growing along the tail in disproportional lengths. This hair is ideal for use on small doubles or trebles where a 'scruffy' appearance is preferred.

Goat hair A popular mobile hair which is easy to tie. It comes in lengths up to 3in (75mm) and as a result is ideal for winging tubes or Waddingtons. It is slightly softer than bucktail and as a result is also very good for smaller flies where a good amount of animation is required, especially in slow flows.

Marabou turkey plumes These turkey feathers have found great favour with legions of stillwater anglers. Nevertheless, most salmon fly tyers have tended to shy away from this wonderful material. The reason for this is that they are very soft and easily damaged; they are, however, exceptionally mobile. If fished through the water using a sink-and-draw retrieve they produce a lovely pulsating action, as the flues expand and contract. I liken the action to that of a swimming jellyfish.

Squirrel tails An extremely popular hair. It is long, soft and straight which makes it ideal as a winging material. Although many fly tyers use it on fairly large flies, I prefer to restrict its use to hooks up to size 8.

Lureflash This has a very mobile action in water, and is similar to marabou in motion. It is a strong, easy material to use, and as a result finds its way into many hairwing salmon patterns to help provide some additional sparkle and mobility.

Twinkle lureflash Similar to the standard lureflash, but has twinkle flecks incorporated into it to provide additional attractiveness.

Krystal flash Very like lureflash, but stiffer. It is also finer, with very fine beads of reflective material incorporated into each strand. Again, very popular with fly dressers to add additional charm to tubes and Waddingtons.

SLF hanks (synthetic living fibre) This is a man-made material distributed by Partridge of Redditch. It was created by the well known Welsh fly tyer Davy Wotton. The long straight fibres from these hanks are suitable for a wide range of applications, and have found favour as a winging and hackling material with many salmon fly dressers. At the time of writing this book the hanks are available in fifteen different colours.

Appendix II
FLY PATTERNS

Ally's Shrimp

Feelers	About a dozen long orange bucktail hair fibres.
Body	Rear half red or orange floss. Front section black floss.
Rib	Oval silver.
Wing	Grey squirrel tail, with GP tippet tied on top.
Hackle	Grey squirrel tail as beard.
Collar	Hot orange hackle.

Arndilly Fancy (favoured by Crawford Little)

Hook	Low-water double.
Tag	Oval silver.
Tail	GP topping.
Body	Yellow floss.
Throat	Bright blue.
Wing	Black.
Cheeks	Jungle cock.
Head	Red.

Black Pennell

Tail	GP topping, or tippets.
Body	Black floss.
Rib	Oval silver.
Hackle	Black cock.
Throat	Black cock tied long.

Blue Charm (tied Wood style)

* Wood-style fly dressings start approximately halfway along shank.

Hook	Low-water single.
Tag	Silver twist.
Tail	GP topping.
Body	Black floss.
Rib	Oval silver.
Wing	Strips of mallard with a thin covering of teal topping.

Bourrach (favoured by Crawford Little)

Hook	Low-water double.
Tag	Oval silver.
Body	Flat Silver.
Rib	Oval silver.
Throat	Blue cock.
Wing	Yellow hair.

Carron (Spey style)

Hook	Original tied on low-water single.
Body	Orange wool.
Rib	Flat silver tinsel, scarlet floss and fine oval silver.
Hackle	Black heron.
Wings	Bronze mallard.
Head	Black.

Collie Dog

Body	Aluminium tube.
Wing	Long black curling hair from behind the rear legs of a black Scottish collie.

Drowned Mouse (invented by Francis Grant)

Tail	Red bucktail all round tube.
Tag	Four or five turns of oval silver twist tinsel.
Rib	Oval silver twist tinsel.
Body	Black floss.
Wing	Yellow bucktail under neath orange, under neath black and round tube.

Elver Fly (invented by Arthur Ransome)

Hook	Low-water double.
Body	Black floss.
Rib	Fine oval silver.
Wing	Two blue vulturine guinea fowl feathers tied back to back.
Collar	Plain blue vulturine.
Cheeks	Jungle cock.
Head	Red.

Garry Dog

Hooks	Doubles, trebles, tubes and Waddingtons.
Tail	GP topping (Only on doubles and trebles).
Tag	Oval silver tinsel (I prefer gold).
Body	Black floss.
Rib	Oval silver floss (I prefer gold).
Throat	Dyed blue guinea-fowl (only on double and

treble hooks, none on tubes or Waddingtons).

Wing	Red under yellow (amounts can be varied to suit different water clarities and personal tastes).

General Practitioner (Invented by Esmond Drury)

* Original tying as given by ED in the summer edition of *Gamefishing & Fly-tying Quarterly*.

Hook	Originally tied on 2/0 double, but later tied on ED trebles down to size 10.
Feelers	About a dozen orange bucktail hairs.
Body	Orange seal's fur.
Legs (body hackle)	Orange cock hackle palmered along body. On the smaller size hooks he would omit the body hackle altogether.
Rib	Oval gold.
Prawn's back	Single GP breast feather tied in at the head and laid along top of hook (this should extend a little beyond the bends of hook).
Eyes	GP tippet with a 'V' section removed from the centre.
Head	Red.

Goat's Toe

Tail	Red wool.
Body	Red seal's fur.
Rib	Bronze peacock herl.
Throat	Long blue peacock.

Hairy Mary Variant (favoured by Francis Grant)

Tag	Four turns of oval silver twist.
Rib	Oval silver twist.
Body	Black floss.
Wing	Mixed natural black and dyed blue; squirrel tail tied all round.

Jungle Buck (invented by Crawford Little)

Hook	Waddington shank.
Tag	Three or four turns of gold oval tinsel.
Tail	Yellow bucktail tied on top and bottom of shank. Should be about length of shank.
Body	Black floss.
Rib	Flat and oval gold tinsel laid side by side.
Wing	Orange bucktail top and bottom taken about 1in past bends of hooks.
Cheeks	Jungle cock.
Head	Black.

Keachie's Krill

Hook	Partridge Wilson doubles code Q2, sizes 8, 10 and 12s.
Tag (optional)	Oval silver tinsel.
Feelers	One golden pheasant breast feather.
Body	Flat Veniard pearl tinsel.
Rib	Oval silver.
Body hackle	Veniard's light claret cock hackle. This should be wound just forward of the middle of the shank. (one to two turns)
Wings	Jungle cock, tied in (optional) traditional shrimp fashion.
Collar hackle	Orange cock (one to two turns).
Head	Black.

Lady Caroline (Spey style)

Tag	None.
Tail	Tip of GP breast feather.
Body	Brown and greeny-olive wool mixed 2 to 1.
Rib	Flat gold and oval silver.
Hackle	Grey heron.
Throat	GP breast feather.
Wing	Bronze mallard, tied pent-style.

Logie (tied Reg Righyni style)

* Tying from an article written by RR which appeared in the autumn edition of *Gamefishing & Fly-tying Quarterly*.

Hook	Low-water single.
Tag	Silver wire.
Rib	Silver wire.
Body	Rear third yellow, front two-thirds black.
Wing	Yellow cock hackle fibre under gingery brown.
Throat	Few strands of blue cock hackle.

March Brown (tied Wood style)

* Wood style fly dressings start halfway away along shank.

Hook	Low-water single.
Tag	Gold twist.
Tail	GP topping.
Body	Finely dubbed hare's ear.
Rib	Oval gold.
Hackle	Teases out body dubbing.
Throat	Partridge.
Wing	Hen pheasant tail.

Munro Killer (favoured by Arthur Oglesby and Crawford Little)

Hook	Low-water double, or treble.
Tag	Oval gold.
Tail	None.
Body	Black floss.
Rib	Gold tinsel.
Throat	Mix of orange cock fibres and blue guinea fowl.
Wing	Black over yellow squirrel. Should be about twice the length of hook. An alternative method is yellow squirrel with black barring.

Silver Blue (tied Wood style)

* Wood-style fly dressings start halfway along shank.

Hook	Low-water single.
Tag	Flat silver.
Tail	GP topping.
Body	Flat silver tinsel.
Rib	Oval silver.
Throat	Blue cock fibres.
Wing	Teal.
Head	Red.

Silver Stoat

Tag	None.
Tail	A few orange hackle fibres.
Body	Flat silver tinsel.
Wing	Black stoat or squirrel tail on top and under shank.

Stoat's Tail

Tail	None.
Rib	Flat silver tinsel.
Body	Black floss.
Wing	Stoat tail hairs, or black squirrel tail.

Thunder and Lightning (tied Reg Righyni style)

* Tying from an article written by RR which appeared in the autumn edition of *Gamefishing and Fly-tying Quarterly.*

Hook	Low-water single.
Tag	Gold wire.
Rib	Gold wire.
Body	Rear third yellow front two thirds black.
Wing	Mix of yellow, brown and maroon cock fibres.
Throat	Blue and orange cock hackles mixed together.

Bibliography

Bridges, Anthony. *Modern Salmon Fishing*, Adam Charles & Black (second edition 1969)

Buckland, John and Oglesby, Arthur. *A Guide to Salmon Flies*, The Crowood Press (1990)

Crossley, Anthony. *The Floating Line for Salmon and Sea Trout*, Methuen Publishers (1939)

Currie, William. *The River Within*, Merlin Urwin Books (1993)

Falkus, Hugh. *Salmon Fishing, A Practical Guide*, H.F.G. Witherby (reprint 1989)

Falkus, Hugh. *Speycasting, A New Technique*, Excellent Press, London (1994)

Grant, Francis. *Salmon Fly Fishing, The Dynamics Approach*, Swanhill Press (1993)

Graesser, Neil. *Advanced Salmon Fishing*, The Boydell Press (reprint 1991)

Knowles, Derek. *Salmon on the Dry Fly*, H.F.G. Witherby Ltd (1987)

Little, Crawford. *The Salmon Fisherman's Year*, Lochar Publishing Ltd (1990)

Little, Crawford. *Success with Salmon*, David & Charles (1988)

Lythgoe, Nicholas John. *The Ecology of Vision*, Oxford University Press (1979)

Mackenzie, Philips. *Successful Modern Salmon Flies*, Blandford Press (1989)

Maunsell, G.W. *The Fisherman's Vade Mecum*, Adam & Charles Black London (1972)

Oglesby, Arthur. *Fly Fishing for Salmon and Sea Trout*, The Crowood Press (1990)

Spencer, Sidney. *Salmon and Seatrout in Wild Places*, H.F.G.Witherby Ltd (1968)

Righyni, Reg. *Advanced Salmon Fishing*, Macdonald General Books (third impression 1980)

Taverner, Scott. Scott and Jock. *Salmon Fishing, Lonsdale Library*, Seeley Services & Co (1972)

Waddington, Richard. *Salmon Fishing, a New Philosophy*, Peter Davies (1947)

Waddington, Richard. *Waddington on Salmon Fishing*, The Crowood Press (1991)

Index